BRIDAL
FINANCIAL BOOT CAMP

A **NEW** way of thinking

PATRICIA B. MULL, CPA, PFS

LifeRich Publishing is a registered trademark of The Reader's Digest Association, Inc.

LifeRich Publishing books may be ordered through booksellers or by contacting:

LifeRich Publishing
1663 Liberty Drive
Bloomington, IN 47403
www.liferichpublishing.com
1 (888) 238-8637

Because of the dynamic nature of the Internet, any web addresses or links contained in this book may have changed since publication and may no longer be valid. The views expressed in this work are solely those of the author and do not necessarily reflect the views of the publisher, and the publisher hereby disclaims any responsibility for them.

This book is a work of non-fiction. Unless otherwise noted, the author and the publisher make no explicit guarantees as to the accuracy of the information contained in this book and in some cases, names of people and places have been altered to protect their privacy.

ISBN: 978-1-4897-2303-1 (sc)
ISBN: 978-1-4897-2301-7 (hc)
ISBN: 978-1-4897-2302-4 (e)

Library of Congress Control Number: 2019906385

Print information available on the last page.

LifeRich Publishing rev. date: 7/11/2019

Table of Contents

The purpose of Bridal Boot Camp is to provide you with information, tools, strategies, and hot tips to help **YOU** preserve **YOUR** wealth if and when you are ever faced with divorce.

I strongly encourage you to read Bridal Financial Boot Camp, if you can, before you get married so that at all times **YOU** are in control of your financial future.

The chances are that you will experience one or even more "Big D" events in your lifetime and unless you are prepared, any divorce can potentially end up being the single most financially devastating event of your lifetime.

You may not always be able to control the circumstances of your relationships, but you can decide to control your financial future. Whether you are in a marriage, about to say I DO or have already proclaimed I DO NOT!, you will do well to learn how to protect yourself from the FINANCIAL RISKS that come both during and after marriage.

YES! when you get married, you are taking on a bundle of FINANCIAL RISKS and if you do not take the management of these risks seriously, they are liable to take you down and take you out financially.

Marriage related risks include both personality and situational risks. For example, there are some personality and addiction problems that you may not discover before you said I DO which can increase your risk of endless financial problems in the future.

- ✔ Substance abuse – drinking and drugs
- ✔ Gambling addiction
- ✔ Laziness and lack of ambition
- ✔ Lies and dishonesty

Other risks and situations that can create financial disasters for you could include situations such as:

- ✔ The unforeseen and uninsured early disability of your spouse.
- ✔ The early or untimely death of your spouse leaving you behind with children, debt and no life insurance or income.
- ✔ Constant and excessive and wasteful spending by your spouse.
- ✔ Bankruptcy caused by bad financial decisions.

The list goes on but the message is clear! Take care and look out for **yourself!**

TRY TO BE FINANCIALLY SELFISH AND INDEPENDENT AT ALL TIMES!

For those of you who have not read my book *The Essentials for Accumulating and Preserving Wealth*, in addition to financial safeguards, strategies, and tax tips for dealing with divorce, in Bridal Financial Boot Camp, you will also be introduced to an entirely **NEW** mindset to help you come to grips with taking control of your financial future now and tomorrow.

NEW is my acronym for **NET WORTH, EQUITY and WEALTH**. These are all one and the same. In Bridal Financial Boot Camp you will learn that a key to successfully planning and surviving a divorce is to keep your eye focused on your **NEW** at all times. This includes **BEFORE, DURING AND AFTER the Big D.**

Although on the outside it may look daunting to accumulate and preserve wealth, there is really no mystery to it.

WEALTH ACCUMULATION

Wealth accumulation is the growth of your NET WORTH, **or as we call it your** NEW. More than just "money in the bank", your NEW is the total value of your property, investments and all other assets less your debts.

 WEALTH PRESERVATION

Wealth preservation is holding on to your accumulated NEW and maintaining it in spite of changing economic conditions and life circumstances that surround you.

 WEALTH MANAGEMENT

Wealth management is the combination of planning principles, strategies and services that help you to accumulate and preserve wealth.

Our Bridal Financial Boot Camp will provide you with a NEW FOCUS and a NEW MINDSET for accumulating and preserving your wealth that you will remember for the rest of your life.

ASSETS – LIABILITIES = **N**et worth = **E**quity = **W**ealth

KEEP YOUR EYE ON THE RED BALL! NEW

Introduction

Normally, a book starts at the beginning and flows through a middle and then on to the end. However, when it comes to marriage and divorce, it is completely opposite because your ultimate focus has got to be on where you end up in the long run. This is hard to do when you are struggling with the emotion of a divorce but you have to force yourself to focus.

So, let us begin with the last thing first and answer the fundamental question of, **"Where do you need to end up?"** Fortunately, the answer is very simple. **RETIRED!**

Single or married – you will retire if you live long enough!

The financial decisions that you make today will shape your financial future of tomorrow and ultimately what your future retirement will look like. You will either have a pleasant retirement or you will end up having a boring and not to mention stressful one. This is up to you! Your choice!

THINK BAG LADY/MAN OR FINANCIALLY SECURE!

Look at retirement as another financial goal BUT, once you are married, realize that it is probably the most important financial goal to which you need to pay attention.

- Let us quickly break Retirement down and analyze WHY you need to pay special attention to your Retirement goal at all times and especially when you are in a marriage

    - ✔ Statistics show that there is a 50% or greater chance that your marriage will end in divorce. Worse, gray divorces are becoming common and so don't think for one minute that "it cannot happen to me"

    - ✔ During your marriage you may save and achieve many goals but the reason that the retirement goal is different is because one day you will be forced to retire! Simple!

    EXAMPLE: A goal may be a boat, a Recreational Vehicle, or even a summer home. If you save and manifest any of these goals that is great but if you don't it is not important in the scheme of things. However, you can't miss the mark with your retirement goal because the day will come when you will surely have to retire.

    - ✔ If you do get a divorce, this is when you will take your hardest financial hit UNLESS you have structured your financial future so that you will not get derailed in the event of a divorce.

    EXAMPLE: You and your spouse retire at around age 65 and at age 67 your spouse tells you that he/she would like a divorce. You cry your little heart out to no avail. Once the divorce is settled, you find yourself in a relatively poor financial situation compared to where you were financially before the divorce. Before the Big D there was enough for two of you to sail through retirement but once the pot was split in two the financial dynamics changed completely and you now find yourself wishing that you had paid more attention to protecting YOUR financial future.

    - ✔ The best protection is to plan for the worst by planning retirement for two and not just one person. Overkill? No! If you both reach 75 and you are still married then Congratulations and Champagne for Everyone!

- Many Risks in life can be mitigated by purchasing insurance. Unfortunately, there is no insurance for recovery from divorce. You are on your own baby! This is why as soon as you can you need to make staying on course and making the protection of your retirement a priority!

- Now you understand WHY this book starts at the END and then meanders through the land mines that you are going to have to maneuver to reach the END again!

- Very importantly, I want to stress that it is YOU, and only YOU, who is responsible for SAVING and INVESTING to meet YOUR Retirement goals.

- As we meander through this book and the face of divorce you will learn why you must not delegate the responsibility for your financial future to anyone else regardless of how much you love and trust that person today.

- By now you are thinking to yourself that you thought marriage was going to be a wonderful partnership where everyone played fair! Yes! It is fine to treat marriage as a partnership and it should be treated as a partnership BUT when it comes to your retirement you cannot let your guard down. You must keep your eyes on where YOU want to end up with or without a spouse. Treat the risk of divorce like any other risk! Very Carefully! have regular check ups to make sure that your Retirement plan is staying on course so that even if divorce strikes it will not derail you!

- Tall order yes – but not an impossible order. If you want to stay on course probably the most important lesson that you need to learn is to have constructive financial conversations with your spouse regularly.

- Again – recognize that marriage brings with it a bundle of uninsurable risks, and when you understand this, it will make sense to you why DIVORCE is just another one of those risks. Unfortunately, divorce is a risk where you are probably going to take your hardest financial hit unless you keep your financial wits about you from the moment you say I DO!

"Bye, Bye, Cinderella and Prince Charming! Hello, Dolly and Fred Astaire!"

HOT TIP: Start off by choosing your financial partner wisely and always understand and measure the impact that each marital financial decision will have on YOUR future financial goal.

HOT TIP: Remember and never forget that money may not be everything but it is right up there with oxygen. You don't want to run out especially during your old age!

NEW FINANCIAL WISDOM

WEEP NO MORE!

This BOOTCAMP is designed to teach you how to protect yourself financially, before, during, and even after a good or bad marriage.

Only you can choose to make a financial difference in your life.

It's <u>YOUR</u> choice.

CHOOSE TO CONTROL YOUR FINANCIAL FUTURE!

The Emotion of

Divorce

THE EMOTION OF DIVORCE

- Divorce is like stubbing your toe. At first it hurts like hell and you cry and cry for a while, but nobody actually dies from it. Once a little time passes, you completely forget all about the pain of the process and start running and playing the game of life all over again!

- During your divorce you will travel a roller coaster of emotion from shock, hurt, and denial to anger and grief. By the end of the ordeal, you will find forgiveness and acceptance instead of wanting to kill the witch or bastard!

- In the meantime, no matter your true emotional state, view the proceedings as if you are negotiating a business deal. You will then put yourself in the proper state of mind to stand up for what is yours, and the entire process will be over faster.

- Studies have shown that negative emotions can influence the negotiation process between divorcing couples. A person filled with guilt is more likely to yield to opposing demands, while a party full of anger is more likely to force a solution by threats. Those who feel shameful tend to avoid negotiation altogether.

I have been both divorced and widowed. The divorce infiltrated and tore at the very core of my heart and soul, and I felt worthless for at least a year or more. I was on an emotional roller coaster the whole time. As I look back, it was the very worst time of my life.

In comparison, becoming a widow after experiencing a divorce was a piece of cake. Everyone felt sorry for me and spoiled me rotten.

Consider this - when you tearfully bury your spouse, that's the end of it. You grieve and cry because you know that it's final. You are usually left with many beautiful memories.

Not so with a divorce! You cry and emotionally bury your spouse but before you know it, they sit back up in the grave! You then have to bury them again, and again, and again, sometimes for twenty years or more if there are children involved!

HOT TIP: Don't forget to use the emotional upheaval of divorce to lose weight!

A NEW Focus

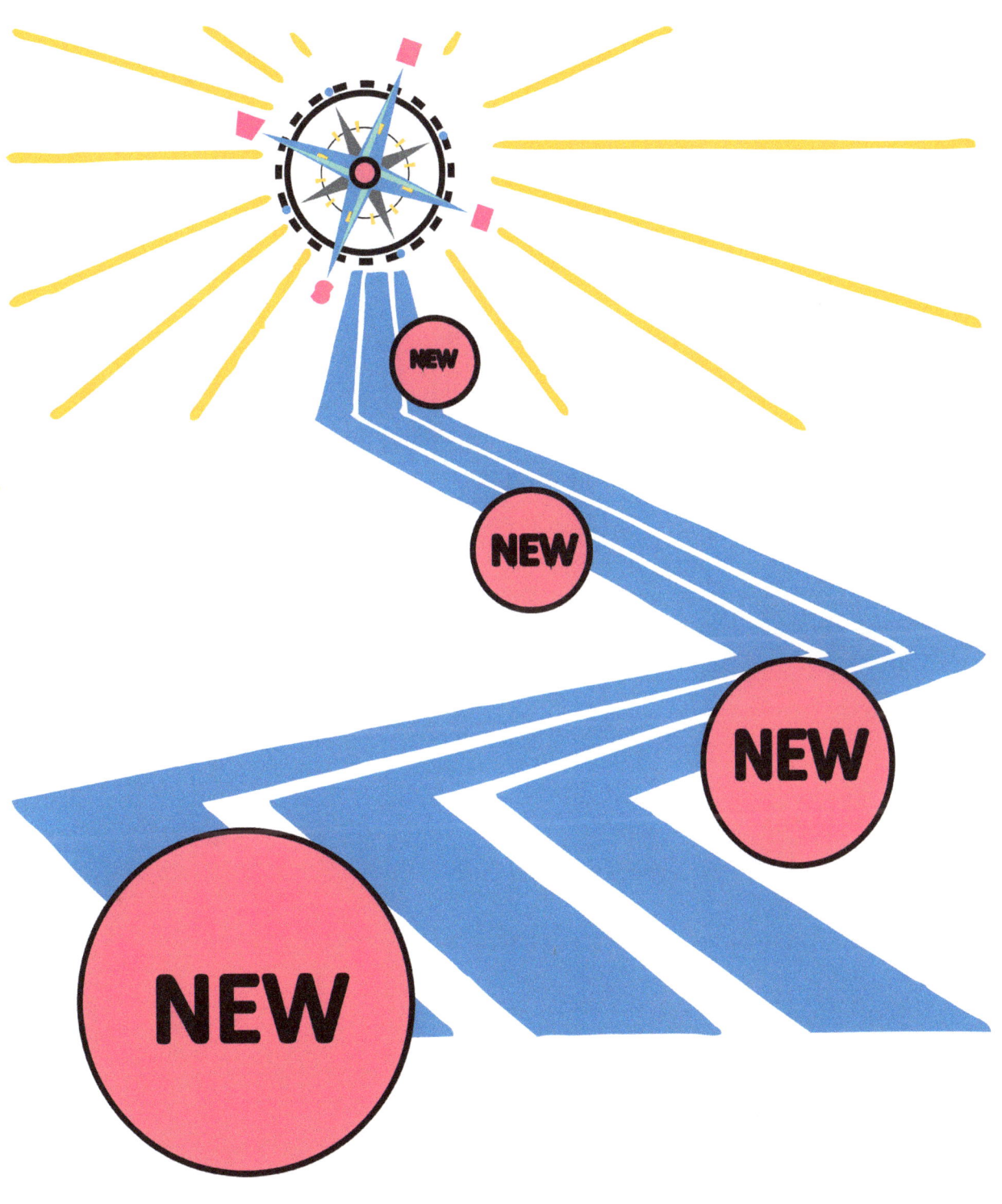

Overview

A NEW Focus Overview

Bridal Financial Boot Camp is divided up in to a series of FOCUSES. Each FOCUS addresses an important financial building block that you will use to create for yourself a secure financial future.

Some of the FOCUSES may contain information that you are already familiar with but try to read the entire content because you just may find one pearl of wisdom in a FOCUS that can provide you with that "Ah Ha" moment that you needed in order to bring other financial pieces in to focus for yourself.

A **NEW FOCUS** ON THE FINANCIAL FACE OF DIVORCE

Bridal Financial Boot Camp's first FOCUS is designed to give you a broad stroke introduction to divorce and how property will be divided in a divorce along with who is "in charge" of a divorce and the various ways of divorce settlements. This FOCUS also introduces you to the concept of Community Property States and Equitable Division States along with the concepts of Marital Assets and Separate Property. It also touches on the types of assets and liabilities that will be divided up and the tax ramifications connected with various assets.

As you travel throughout the rest of Bridal Financial Boot Camp try to keep this basic divorce information in mind.

A **NEW FOCUS** ON RETIREMENT INCOME

Having introduced you to the Face of Divorce and how assets and debts will be divided in a divorce, Bridal Financial Boot Camp now jumps right in to a discussion and FOCUS about the Face of your Retirement and where your retirement income will come from. Why? Because this is key information for you to know and understand so that you can eventually end up as a financial winner versus a financial victim in the future. Information in this Focus can help you stay financially focused during your entire lifetime. Single or Married. Divorce or no Divorce!

A **NEW FOCUS** ON UNDERSTANDING YOUR NET WORTH

NEW is an acronym for **Net Worth, Equity and Wealth**. These are all one and the same!

This FOCUS begins the conversation and lays the foundation for you to understand your **NEW** and how to grow your **NEW**. Once you are in control of the simplicity of what increases and decreases your **NEW** you are on your way!

Single or married you need to understand your **NEW** and how to grow your **NEW**.

A **NEW FOCUS** ON ACCUMULATING WEALTH

In this FOCUS you will gain insight and understanding about the fundamental building blocks building blocks for accumulating **NEW**

YOU EARN
YOU SAVE
YOU INVEST
YOU ACCUMULATE.

It is that simple!

A NEW Focus Overview

A **NEW FOCUS** ON SETTING GOALS AND BUDGETING

This FOCUS will help you to understand budgeting and the positive impact that a budget can have on helping you to materialize your financial goals.

A budget is not a set of handcuffs! A budget is an important tool for you to use in connection with building your **NEW**.

Budgeting is especially important when you are married because it is a great way to keep tabs on wasteful spending and also on how **YOUR** half of the family **NEW** is growing!

A **NEW FOCUS** ON MANAGING DEBT

Using debt is a substitute for using cash and can destroy your **NEW**. Remember always that debt decreases your **NEW**.

This FOCUS will help you understand more about debt and provide you with useful strategies such as using a budget for minimizing the use of debt. You will also better understand why interest expense is so toxic to your **NEW**.

A **NEW FOCUS** ON PROTECTING YOUR **NEW**

This FOCUS is all about protecting and holding on to your **NEW** and reasons why you have to guard it at all times.

As long as you have **NEW**, someone will be making it their business to try to put your **NEW** in their pocket!

A **NEW FOCUS** ON TIME, INFLATION AND PURCHASING POWER

TIPP – TIME, INFLATION AND PURCHASING POWER will always be with us. This is why it is so important for you to understand these 3 amigos and how to make them your friend versus your enemy!

A **NEW FOCUS** ON DIVORCE ISSUES AND STRATEGIES

In this FOCUS Bridal Financial Boot Camp brings the conversation full circle back to more divorce issues and strategies. This FOCUS introduces concepts such as alimony, child support, social security, bankruptcy, income taxes, death and other useful information that you can keep in the back of your mind. Some of the information may seem repetitive but it is included again to provide reinforcement.

A **NEW FOCUS** ON THE COST OF DIVORCE

So, how much does a divorce cost?

It is not only the cost of the attorney that hurts. It is also the other costs related to endless appraisals and court costs and other costs that can quickly add up. After a while, it seems as if the divorce has taken on a life of its own and become a money pit. You will learn more about these costs in this FOCUS.

Sorry – but do NOT try to do the divorce yourself on the internet! This is a very bad idea.

A NEW Focus Overview

A **NEW FOCUS** ON FINANCIAL PERSONALITIES

Bridal Financial Boot Camp next brings in to FOCUS and analyzes different financial personalities and attempts to provide you with insight in to the different financial personalities that can work well with your financial personality versus those personalities that will not.

Many financial personalities will simply keep putting bad dents in your hard earned **NEW** even to the point of totally destroying your financial future.

A **NEW FOCUS** ON FINANCIAL PREDATORS

Financial Predators are everywhere and their game plan is always trying to steal your **NEW**.

This FOCUS is designed to help you identify their techniques and clever ways and provide you with the tools that you need to put **YOU** in control when you find yourself being attacked by a predator.

A **NEW FOCUS** ON BANANAS

You can't straighten out a Banana! This FOCUS is designed to help you recognize the Bananas in your life and give you the courage to deal with them!

A **NEW FOCUS** ON IDENTIFYING CAPABLE PROFESSIONALS

If you have an inkling that you may be heading down the path towards a divorce, it's good to know how to find the right professionals for your team. This FOCUS is designed to help you with this. Just remember that it's not necessarily the best pit bull professional who wins the day for you in a divorce – it more often than not is the best poker player.

A **NEW FOCUS** ON YOUR RESPONSIBILITIES

The days of trying to blame someone else for your financial mistakes, messes and missed targets are over. **YOU** have got to take responsibility for building your financial independence, your financial future and your **NEW**. By just following some simple rules and paying attention to consistently growing your **NEW**, the chances are that you will do far better in the long run than the average person.

A NEW Focus Overview

LEARNING FROM REAL LIFE TRICKS AND TRAGEDIES

There is nothing better than real life experiences to reinforce the risks and realities embedded in marriage! Love may be blind but that does not mean that you have to be financially blindsided! This FOCUS is designed to help you stay alert and teach you that it is all right for you to put your foot down when you have to. Nothing says that you have to be another financial failure statistic! Keep building your **NEW** and don't let anyone stand in your way! Keep your eye on that Red Ball!

GOODBYE IS YOUR NEW BEGINNING

We never say Goodbye.

Even our Goodbye FOCUS contains great wisdom for you!

CHECKLISTS

Finally, Bridal Financial Boot Camp provides you several financial checklists that will keep you headed in the right direction!

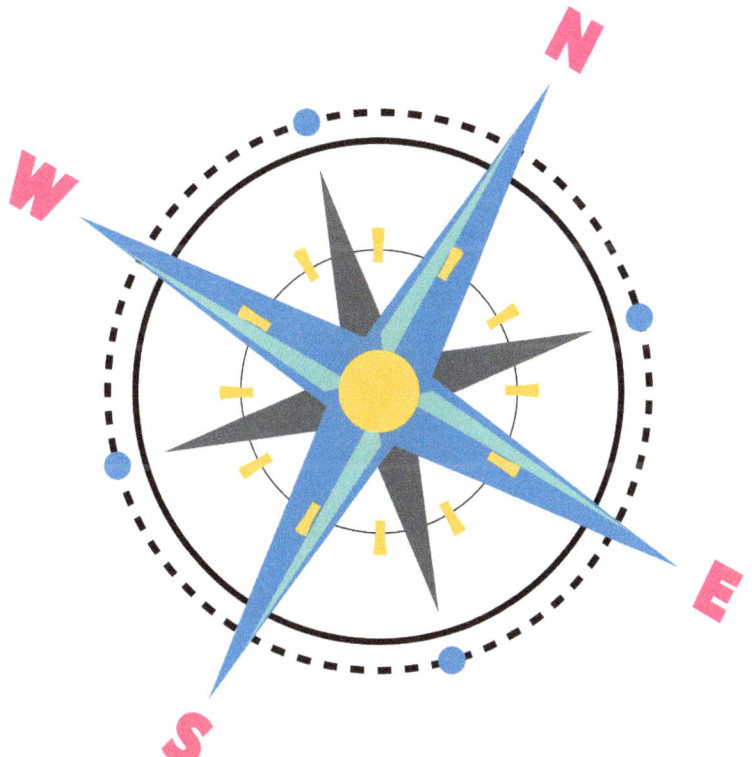

NEW FINANCIAL WISDOM

DON'T LET DIVORCE MAKE BOTH AN EMOTIONAL AND FINANCIAL CRIPPLE OUT OF YOU!

Make it your business to understand how the financial mechanics of divorce works in your State

and

Stay alert financially throughout your marriage!

Always have a solid financial bailout emergency strategy for yourself and your children

NEVER LET YOUR GUARD DOWN

A NEW Focus on

50% ?   50% ?

The Financial
Face of Divorce

INTRODUCTION A NEW FOCUS ON THE FINANCIAL FACE OF DIVORCE

🐚 **INTRODUCTION**

🐚 **STATE LAWS**

🐚 **TYPES OF WAYS TO REACH A "SETTLEMENT"**

🐚 **THE FINAL DIVORCE DECREE**

🐚 **CLASSIFICATION OF PROPERTY IN A DIVORCE**

🐚 **ASSETS AND LIABILITIES THAT WILL BE DIVIDED**

Bridal Financial Boot Camp's first FOCUS is designed to give you a broad stroke introduction to divorce and how property will be divided in a divorce along with who is "in charge" of a divorce and the various ways of divorce settlements. This FOCUS also introduces you to the concept of Community Property States and Equitable Division States along with the concepts of Marital Assets and Separate Property. It also touches on the types of assets and liabilities that will be divided up and the tax ramifications connected with various assets.

As you travel throughout the rest of Bridal Financial Boot Camp try to keep this basic divorce information in mind.

They say marriages are made
in Heaven.
But, so is thunder and lightning!
—*Clint Eastwood*

Let's get started!

OVERVIEW

- Even in the happiest relationships, divorce is too big a risk to ignore.

- Did you know the odds of a hurricane hitting the Florida Keys are around 27%? The likelihood of a first marriage ending in divorce is 45-50%. For second marriages, 67% end in divorce, and third marriages are even more dismal at 73%.

- Divorce is all too often the life event that causes women to take their hardest financial hit. They are usually not prepared either emotionally or financially for divorce and often bear most of the responsibility for child care cost while facing a reduced earning potential compared to their male counterparts. Some recover; but more often than not, women who are ill prepared find themselves in a devastating position. This makes it imperative that you understand the rules of how divorce works.

- Never let your financial guard down during your marriage. Always know where you are financially and what your property rights are and how divorce works.

- Please do NOT be the person who comes to me and says, "I just wish that I had paid more attention to my financial future."

> **Marriage communication starting to go downhill:** A couple drove down a country road for several miles, not saying a word. An earlier discussion had led to an argument and neither of them wanted to concede his position. As they passed a barnyard of mules, goats, and pigs, the husband asked sarcastically, "Relatives of yours?" "Yep," said the wife replied, "in-laws."

 STATE LAW GOVERNS:

- ✔ Property & Income Settlement
- ✔ Division of Assets & Liabilities tax etc.
- ✔ Alimony
- ✔ Child Support
- ✔ Miscellaneous related issues such as income

 TYPES OF WAYS TO REACH A "SETTLEMENT":

- ✔ No attorney – draft own documents (extremely foolish)
- ✔ Negotiated friendly (Is there such a thing?)
- ✔ Negotiated not-so-friendly (May be able to reach settlement via mediation.)
- ✔ Settlement by private judge (Great choice but you must agree and have no minor children)
- ✔ Go to court and let judge make decision – EXPENSIVE!

FINAL DIVORCE DECREE

- ✔ The divorce settlement is finalized and spouses go their separate ways.

NOTES

CLASSIFICATION OF PROPERTY IN A DIVORCE

Assets are divided according to State Law, so the starting point is determining if you live in a Community Property State or if you live in an Equitable Division State. Know your rights!

COMMUNITY PROPERTY STATES

- Community Property States recognize a 50% ownership right in each property. Property is generally divided 50/50.

- Alaska, Arizona, California, Idaho, Louisiana, New Mexico, Nevada, Texas, Washington, Wisconsin, Puerto Rico.

EQUITABLE DIVISION STATES

- Most states follow the equitable division of property whereby both parties negotiate a fair division of property with their attorneys. If an agreement can not be reached, a judge will handle the dispute.

Within these two categories property is again divided and classified as follows:

MARITAL PROPERTY

- Marital property is property acquired during the marriage and usually excludes gifts and inheritances unless these have been commingled.

- Marital assets are generally divided between the spouses.

SEPARATE PROPERTY

- Separate property is property that you bring into the marriage and also includes gifts and inheritances received during the marriage.

- In most states property which has been kept separate and not commingled, is not subject to division but again, you must recognize that each State has it's own peculiar laws and exceptions along with interpretations and therefore you must make it your business to know the state law rights in the state where you are residing to make sure that you know what legal rights you have in every asset whether it is held separately or jointly.

TAKE AWAY: The time to find out about your current and future rights in each and every one of your assets and the assets that you will build within your marriage is BEFORE you get married. If you want to build wealth, this is fundamental must know information.

TAKE AWAY: If you want to guarantee an asset in your marriage as separate property, don't depend on State Law. Get a pre-marital or post-marital agreement signed. In the meantime, DO NOT commingle money received from gifts and inheritances. Keep it in your own name and separate.

NOTES

ASSETS AND LIABILITIES THAT WILL BE DIVIDED

EXAMPLES OF ASSETS THAT WILL BE DIVIDED	EXAMPLES OF LIABILITIES TO BE RESOLVED BETWEEN SPOUSES

EXAMPLES OF ASSETS THAT WILL BE DIVIDED

* Cash
* Personal Residence and Other Real Estate
* Brokerage Accounts & marketable securities
* Employer Retirement Plans
* Individual Retirement Accounts
* Family Business
* Partnership Interests
* Cash Surrender Value of Life Insurance
* Copyrights & trademarks
* Jewelry
* Boats
* All Vehicles
* Pets
* Annuities
* Installment Notes
* Mortgage Notes Receivable

EXAMPLES OF LIABILITIES TO BE RESOLVED BETWEEN SPOUSES

* Unsecured debt
  * ✔ Credit Cards
  * ✔ Unsecured personal notes

* Secured debt
  * ✔ Mortgages on Real Estate
  * ✔ Tax Debt
  * ✔ Other Secured Notes such as auto and boat loans

1 Basically, everything owned by a couple is subject to division in a divorce unless it is legally deemed to be separate property or is part of a prenuptial agreement. At the beginning of the divorce process, both parties prepare a list of all of their assets, liabilities, income and expenses before the division can begin.

2 The value of these assets are finally determined by qualified appraisers.

3 Each asset has its own income tax characteristics with respect to the income that it generates and also with respect to distributions on the partial or complete liquidation of the asset. You should try to become knowledgeable about these because, when negotiating a fair and equitable settlement, tax differences should be recognized and taken into consideration during negotiation. An example of this is that $100,000 sitting in a traditional IRA is worth less than $100,000 sitting in a bank account. Why? the IRA has a nasty "built-in" income tax that you must pay to the IRS when you distribute it. The cash sitting in the bank account is free and clear of all taxes. They are not equal!

4 Secured debt in a divorce attaches itself to the asset that it is securing.

NOTES

THOUGHTS AND CONVERSATIONS for PROTECTING YOUR NEW

Question: Do you know if you are living in a Community Property State or an Equitable Division State?

Question: Do you understand that any asset that you bring in to the marriage or even acquire during the marriage (think automobile) may be subject to division in the event of a divorce?

Question: Have you considered entering in to a pre-nuptial agreement to protect property that you are bringing in to the marriage from being deemed marital property in the event of a divorce?

Question: Do you know what assets and liabilities your fiancé is bringing in to the marriage and whether or not any of the assets will be treated as separate property?

Question: Are you protecting YOUR separate property that you bring in to your marriage by keeping it in your own name after your marriage and not comingling it in any way with marital assets?

Question: Do you understand the tax liability ramification of signing a joint income tax return with your spouse?

A NEW Focus on

Retirement Income

A NEW FOCUS ON RETIREMENT INCOME

- SOURCES OF RETIREMENT INCOME

- HOW TO QUICKLY ESTIMATE RETIREMENT NEEDS

- RETIREMENT IS AN AMOUNT, NOT AN AGE

- DO YOU HAVE ENOUGH INCOME?

- DIVORCES AND YOUR NEW

Having introduced you to the Face of Divorce and how assets and debts will be divided in a divorce, Bridal Financial Boot Camp now jumps right in to a discussion and FOCUS about the Face of your Retirement and where your retirement income will come from. Why? Because this is key information for you to know and understand so that you can eventually end up as a financial winner versus a financial victim in the future. Information in this Focus can help you stay financially focused during your entire lifetime. Single or Married. Divorce or no Divorce!

Let's get started!

EXAMPLES OF SOURCES OF RETIREMENT INCOME

First, let us look at some typical SOURCES of your future retirement income. An understanding of these sources will help you lay the foundation for understanding what you need to focus on during your working career in order financially prepare yourself for retirement.

%	SOURCE OF INCOME	EXAMPLES	RISK
	SOCIAL SECURITY	Do not avoid contributions to Social Security	+
	LIFETIME GUARANTEED INCOME (Governmental and Non-Government Source)	• Corporate or Private Pensions • Variaw ble Annuities • Fixed Annuities	++
	BONDS & FIXED INCOME INVESTMENTS	• Individual Corporate Bonds and Municipal Bonds • Mutual Funds, Exchange Traded Funds and Closed End Funds containing Corporate and Municipal Bonds securities and other debt securities	++
	STOCKS WITH DIVIDENDS	• Large Cap Stock and other equities with growth potential and dividend paying ability • Preferred Stock, Reits, MLPs	+++
	ALTERNATIVE INVESTMENTS	• Real Estate Income, • Equipment Leasing Income, • Hedge Funds • Precious Metals • Structured products • Managed Futures • Private Equity • Credit Derivatives.	++++

MARRIED OR SINGLE, AS EARLY AS YOU CAN, START FOCUSING ON YOUR RETIREMENT INCOME AND WHERE THAT FUTURE INCOME WILL COME FROM.

NOTES

HOW TO QUICKLY ESTIMATE RETIREMENT INCOME

Next, let us take a quick look at a very simplified method to quickly estimate how much you will need to save in order to provide yourself with the lifestyle that you want in the future.

As explained later on, there are many factors that need to be taken into consideration when calculating the annual income that you will need when you retire. However, arriving at an approximate amount that you need to save will provide a greater appreciation of HOW to accumulate and preserve wealth.

WHERE WILL MY INCOME COME FROM AT RETIREMENT?	
SOCIAL SECURITY INCOME	$15,000
INCOME FROM PENSION	$10,000
INCOME FROM RETIREMENT PLANS	$30,000
INCOME FROM ANNUITIES	$10,000
BONDS & FIXED INCOME INVESTMENTS	$5,000
STOCKS WITH DIVIDENDS	$5,000
ALTERNATIVE INVESTMENTS	
TOTAL MAKE UP OF RETIREMENT FUNDS	$75,000

ESTIMATED SAVINGS USING A 4% DISTRIBUTION RATE	
SOCIAL SECURITY INCOME	
INCOME FROM PENSION	
INCOME FROM RETIREMENT PLANS	$750,000
INCOME FROM ANNUITIES	$250,000
BONDS & FIXED INCOME INVESTMENTS	$125,000
STOCKS WITH DIVIDENDS	$125,000
ALTERNATIVE INVESTMENTS	
TOTAL MAKE UP OF RETIREMENT FUNDS	$1,250,000

❋ 4% may be too aggressive a distribution rate for your retirement. In this example, inflation has not been taken into consideration and this could seriously impact the purchasing power of your retirement income. Always consult with your financial advisor when planning for your retirement.

NOTES

RETIREMENT IS AN AMOUNT AND NOT AN AGE
WHEN YOU HAVE ENOUGH INCOME TO RETIRE, YOU RETIRE!

Too many rely on their Social Security benefit to be the largest percentage of their retirement income a they do not save. Social Security was never designed to play this dominant role in anyone's nt. It was designed to be a safety net.

Regardless, you did invest in Social Security over the years and you certainly deserve a decent return on that investment. Will it still be there? Chances are that it will still be around because the Government will undoubtedly print the money to meet the obligation. Suffice to say that Social Security is only one part of the financial puzzle that you will have to juggle in order to retire. So, the earlier you start planning your retirement income, the easier it will be for you to reach your retirement goals.

DO NOT LET DIVORCE DERAIL YOU!

Just remember that if you find yourself in a situation where you are going to be forced to depend heavily on Social Security to meet your financial needs during retirement then it may be far smarter financially to wait until you have reached the age of 70 before starting your Social Security benefits. Included in Bridal Financial Boot Camp is a nice piece on Social Security and so we won't deal with this subject in detail here.

A good philosophy is to earn, save, invest, and accumulate on your own, and then let Social Security be an added bonus when you receive it.

The biggest benefit of reaching age 65 is your ability to receive Medicare! If you are going to retire before Age 65 then you have to find affordable medical coverage. Do not go naked! You just may find yourself back in the workforce!

Remember that your retirement income will mostly come from:
- ✔ Income derived from YOU, YOUR efforts, and YOUR investments.
- ✔ Social Security.
- ✔ Do not count on gifts, inheritances, or winning the lottery!

NOTES

DO I HAVE ENOUGH INCOME?

EXAMPLE: You work for a large Corporation and at age 55 you are eligible to receive $5,000 a month plus medical benefits for the rest of your life. Your house is paid for and the children are out of college and this is all of the money that you need to support yourself and family comfortably.

✔ You can retire if you want to retire! Later when you collect social security, look at this as just a bonus!
IMPORTANT QUESTION: What happens if you have to split that pension with an ex-spouse? This is what Bridal Financial Boot Camp is all about! Preparing you for the expected and the unexpected!

EXAMPLE: Alternatively, you are a saver and by age 55 although you do not have a monthly pension, you have paid off your home, the children are all educated and you have no debt and on top of everything you already have a total of $1,300,000 saved. This consists of your 401K plan and your brokerage account that has done well over the years.

✔ If you feel comfortable with this situation you can retire! However, you must make sure that you have full medical coverage because a serious illness before age 65 could put a large dent in your retirement and even put you back into the workforce.
IMPORTANT QUESTION: Again, what now if you have to split your 401K plan and your brokerage account with an ex-spouse who just took on a penniless boyfriend? Ouch!

✔ Again, too many people rely on their Social Security benefit to be the largest percentage of their retirement income and so they do not save. Social Security was not designed to play this dominant role in anyone's retirement.

NOTES

DIVORCES AND YOUR NEW

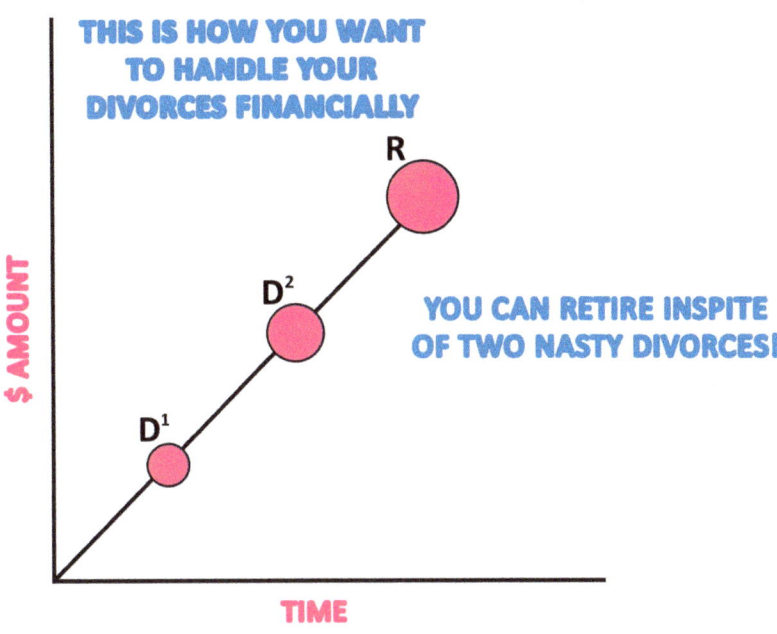

THIS IS HOW YOU WANT TO HANDLE YOUR DIVORCES FINANCIALLY

YOU CAN RETIRE INSPITE OF TWO NASTY DIVORCES!

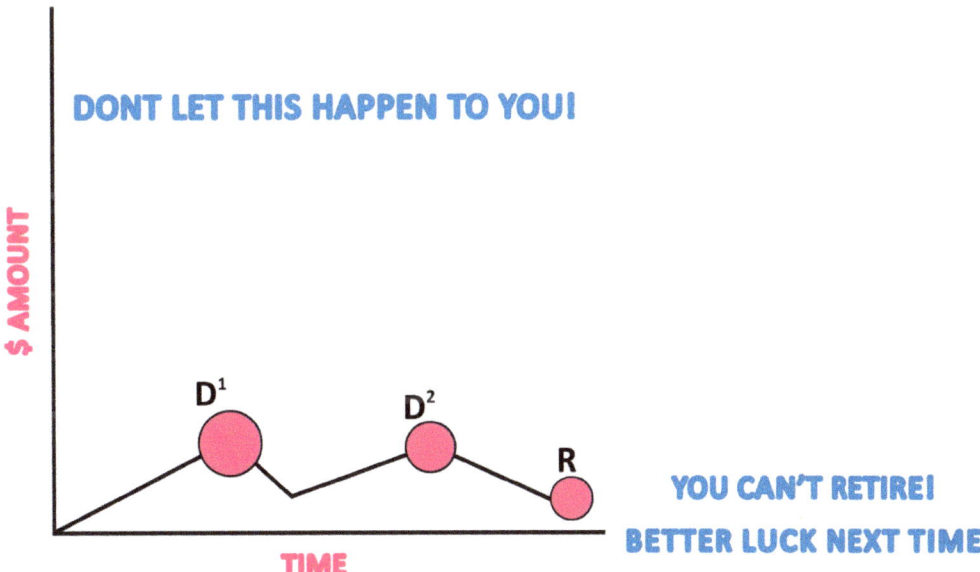

DONT LET THIS HAPPEN TO YOU!

YOU CAN'T RETIRE! BETTER LUCK NEXT TIME

NOTES

THOUGHTS AND CONVERSATIONS for PROTECTING YOUR NEW

Questions: Have you given serious consideration to YOUR retirement needs and where YOUR personal retirement income will come from?

Question: Have you estimated how much you will need to save to meet your retirement goals whether you find yourself married or unmarried when you retire?

Question: Have you made a decision to own and take control of the outcome
of YOUR personal retirement income and not leave it to luck or happenstance?
If not, why not?

Question: Have you had a conversation with your fiancé or spouse about your retirement goals and how you all will budget and save for retirement?

Question: Have you considered how your retirement goals will be impacted by the death or disability of your spouse? What are your strategies to combat this?

Question: Have you considered how your retirement goals will be impacted by a divorce?

Question: Given the alarming odds that any marriage will end in a divorce, have you come to grips with taking responsibility for planning for your own successful retirement so that divorce does not derail you? If not, why not?

A NEW Focus on

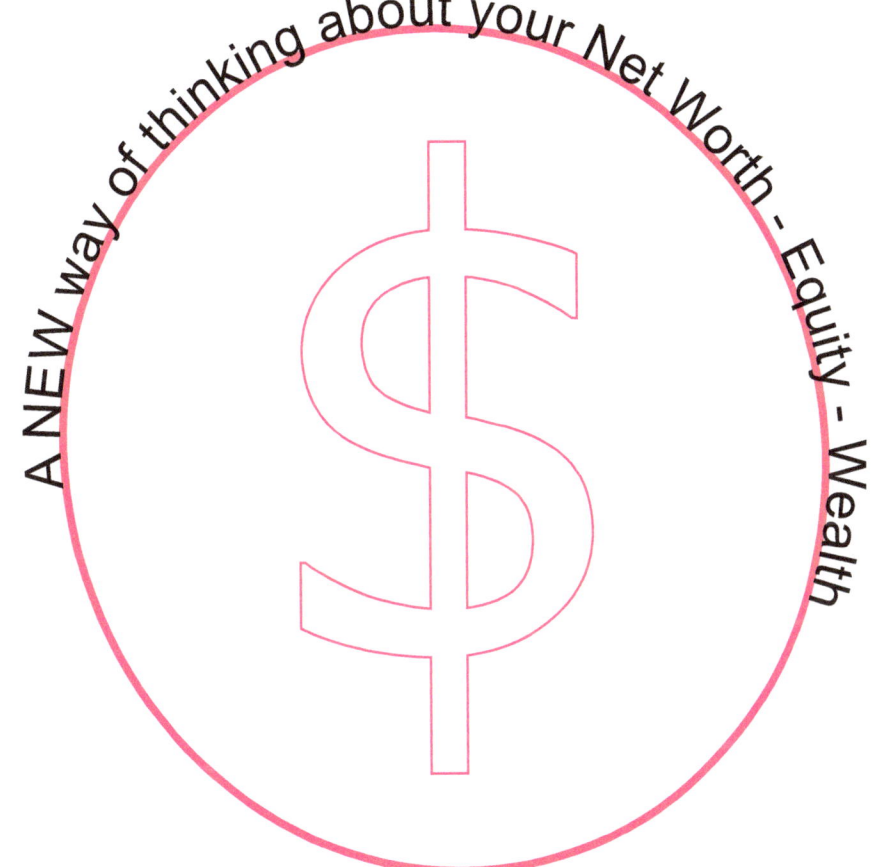

A NEW way of thinking about your Net Worth - Equity - Wealth

Understanding Your Net Worth

A **NEW** FOCUS ON UNDERSTANDING YOUR NET WORTH

- **UNDERSTANDING THE BASICS OF WEALTH**

- **ASSETS AND THE IMPACT ON YOUR NEW**

- **LIABILITIES AND THE IMPACT ON YOUR NEW**

- **CALCULATING YOUR NEW**

- **SUMMING IT UP**

NEW is an acronym for **Net Worth, Equity and Wealth**. These are all one and the same!

This FOCUS begins the conversation and lays the foundation for you to understand your **NEW** and how to grow your **NEW**. Once you are in control of the simplicity of what increases and decreases your **NEW** you are on your way!

Single or married you need to understand your **NEW** and how to grow your **NEW**.

Let's get started!

QUESTION: How will you be able to reach your saving goals, even in the FACE OF DIVORCE?

ANSWER: With the right approach! The most important tool that you need in your tool box is an understanding of how to accumulate and preserve your wealth and stay financially independent regardless of your marital status!

UNDERSTANDING THE BASICS OF WEALTH

As we saw earlier, understanding how assets and liabilities are divided in a divorce is very important. However, the KEY to building up and protecting YOUR wealth, is fundamental to your future financial success.

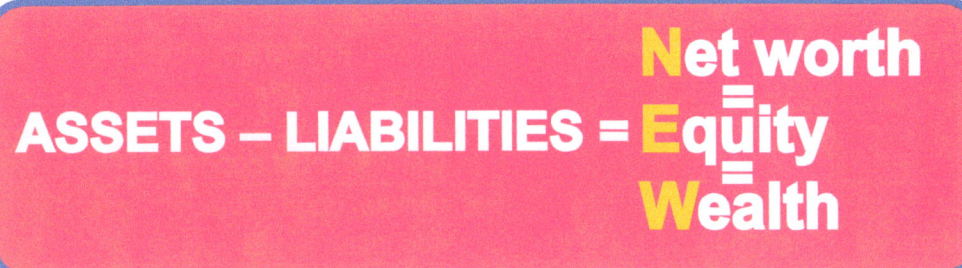

ASSETS – LIABILITIES = **E**quity
Net worth = **E**quity = **W**ealth

🐚 **ASSETS – LIABILITIES = NEW**

Your wealth is the difference between what you own and what you owe.
Example: $10,000 cash – $2,000 owed in credit cards. YOUR **NEW** = $8,000

🐚 **INCREASING NEW IS THE KEY TO INCREASING YOUR WEALTH**

KEY: The very essence of accumulating wealth is to keep growing your **NEW** year by year.

🔹 Bridal Financial Boot Camp has been written to help you understand how to accumulate and preserve your **NEW** regardless of where your journey is beginning.

KEY: The KEY to wealth accumulation is keeping your eye on your **NEW** and using the tools and strategies taught in this book to keep increasing the size of your **NEW**.

🐚 **HOW DO YOU INCREASE YOUR NEW?**

Increase your assets or *decrease y*our liabilities. Simple, but not necessarily easy!

NOTES

ASSETS ARE WHAT YOU OWN.

INCREASING ASSETS ↑ INCREASES ↑ NEW

DECREASING ASSETS ↓ DECREASES ↓ NEW

EXAMPLES OF ASSETS	
LIQUID ASSETS Cash in the Bank and Savings	■ Checking account ■ Money market accounts ■ Savings accounts ■ Cash reserve fund ■ Certificates of deposit
INVESTMENTS Non-Retirement Plan Assets	■ Stocks, bonds, mutual funds, and other securities
Qualified Retirement Plan Accounts	■ Traditional retirement account (IRA) ■ Roth IRA ■ Simple IRA ■ Simplified employee pension (SEP) ■ 401K, 403(b) & 457 plans ■ Deferred annuities ■ Pension profit sharing plans
Real Estate	■ Principal residence ■ Rental real estate ■ Raw land
Other Investments	■ Loans to family & friends ■ Collectibles & artwork ■ Antiques ■ Precious metals ■ Jewelry
DEPRECIABLE CONSUMER PRODUCTS	■ Automobile ■ Boat ■ Home entertainment equipment
OTHER ASSETS	■ Cash surrender value of life insurance

NOTES

LIABILITIES ARE WHAT YOU OWE

LIABILITIES ARE ALSO KNOWN AS DEBT OR LOANS

INCREASING ↑ LIABILITIES DECREASES ↓ NEW

DECREASING ↓ LIABILITIES INCREASES ↑ NEW

DEBT = **LOANS** = **LIABILITIES**

UNSECURED LOANS

- Credit cards
- Loans from family and friends
- Bank seasonal lines of credit
- Personal bank loans

SECURED LOANS

- Automotive loans
- Boat loans
- Furniture loans
- Education loans
- Home improvement loans
- First or second home mortgages

NOTES

A New Focus on Understanding Your Net Worth

❋ Computing and thinking about your overall **NEW** regularly and before you make a financial decision has to become your **NEW MINDSET**! Every time you have to make an expenditure think, "How is this decision going to impact my **NEW**?"

❋ There is no set method for computing your **NEW**, you simply have to find a way to estimate the value of your assets and liabilities. After that you simply subtract your liabilities from your assets.

TIP: Save your computation worksheets so that you can see how your **NEW** is growing over the years!

ASSETS - LIABILITIES

CASH & CASH EQUIVALENTS

Checking account	$_____
Savings account	$_____
Cash reserve savings account	$_____
Money market account	$_____
Certificates of deposits	$_____

NON RETIREMENT ASSETS FOR INVESTMENT

Stocks, bonds and other securities	$_____
outside of retirement accounts	$_____
Precious metals	$_____
Coin collections	$_____
Limited partnerships interests	$_____
Real estate investment trusts	$_____
Hedge funds	$_____
Private equity	

RETIREMENT PLAN ASSETS — $_____

Individual retirement account (IRA)	$_____
Roth IRA	$_____
Simple IRA	$_____
Simplified employee pension (SEP)	$_____
401K & 403b type plans	$_____
Deferred fixed annuities	$_____
Deferred variable annuities	

REAL ESTATE — $_____

Principal residence	$_____
Vacation property	$_____
Rental real estate	

OTHER ASSETS — $_____

Money owed to you	$_____
CSV on life insurance policies	$_____
Autos	$_____
Boats	$_____
Furniture/appliances	$_____ **NOTES**
Jewelry	$_____
Collectibles/artwork	$_____
Other	

TOTAL ASSETS: $_____

LIABILITIES

CREDIT CARD DEBT	$_____
PERSONAL LOANS	$_____
AUTO/BOAT LOANS	$_____
EDUCATION LOANS	$_____
INVESTMENT LOANS	$_____
LIFE INSURANCE LOANS	$_____
MORTGAGES	$_____
OTHER	$_____

TOTAL LIABILITIES: $_____

TOTAL ASSETS: $_____

LESS TOTAL LIABILITIES: $_____

NEW: $_____

You must keep your **FOCUS** on your **NEW**! Use the attached worksheet and set it up on an excel spreadsheet. Customize this for your own use. We have simply included as many items as we could so you do not forget any. You may also use a free online service. Just do it often and enjoy watching your **NEW** grow.

SUMMING IT UP

Earn Save Invest Accumulate + **Set Goals Budget Manage Debt Protect your NEW** + **Time Inflation Purchasing Power** = **NEW Growth**

Understanding these fundamental building blocks, strategies and forces and the relationships of these to your **NEW** will provide you with the tools that you need to reach your financial goals..

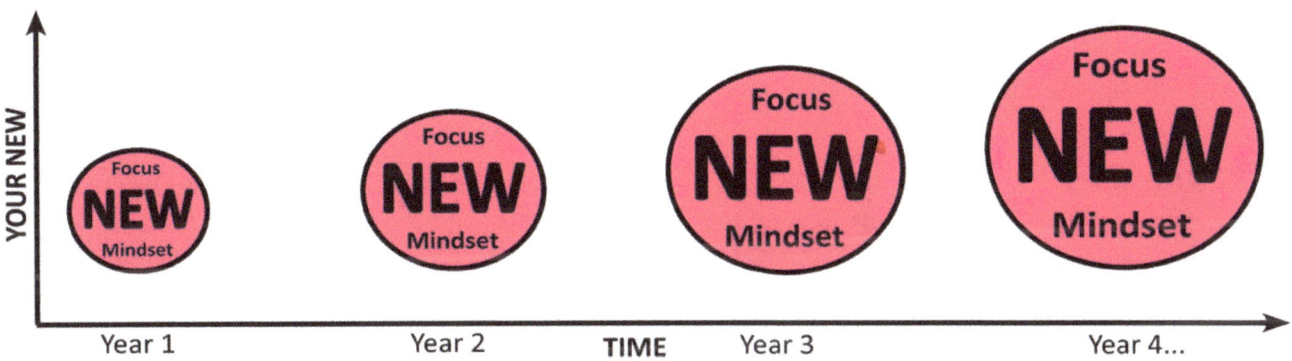

This is how growing your **NEW** is meant to work. Stay **FOCUSED** and it will grow!

NOTES

THOUGHTS AND CONVERSATIONS for PROTECTING YOUR NEW

Question: Have you ever computed your **NEW**?

Question: What is **YOUR NEW** right now?

Question: Do you consider it useful to compute your **NEW** regularly so that you can make sure that it is growing?

Question: What is the **NEW** of your fiancé?

Question: What assets does your fiancé own and what liabilities does he owe?

Question: Do you understand that assets increase your **NEW** and that liabilities decrease your **NEW**?

Question: Have you reviewed your liabilities and come up with a plan to pay them off as soon as you can?

Question: Have you given consideration to how you can earn more?

Question: Have you given consideration to how you can save more?

A NEW Focus on

Accumulating Wealth

A **NEW** FOCUS ON ACCUMULATING WEALTH

🐚 **EARNINGS**

🐚 **YOUR NEW AND YOUR EDUCATION (AVERAGE LIFETIME EARNINGS)**

🐚 **SAVINGS**

🐚 **SAVING STRATEGIES**

🐚 **INVESTING AND ACCUMULATING YOUR NEW**

In this FOCUS you will gain insight and understanding about the fundamental building blocks for accumulating **NEW**

YOU EARN
YOU SAVE
YOU INVEST
YOU ACCUMULATE.

It is that simple!

Let's get started!

...RNINGS

Whether you are single, engaged, or m........ e of the main cornerstones for building your **NEW** is **YOUR** earning power.

The growth of a person's **NEW** is usuall......... to their earning capacity.

A higher earning capacity leads to a per........ ..ility to save more, invest more and ultimately accumulate more.

Sources of earnings include:

- A person's salary
- Income from a trade, business or profession
- Royalty income from patents or copyrighted material
- Income from investments
- Any other effort that generates cash flow such as hobbies

BOTTOM LINE: It pays for you to develop your earning potential to the highest level that you can afford to attain.

On the next page there is a graphic that shows the expected earning capacity for people at various levels of education. This does not mean that just because you do not have a college education that you can't end up with a nice big juicy **NEW**. Quite to the contrary! There are countless of people in trades and other areas of work that have been very successful without the benefit of a college degree. For the average person, however, education makes it easier to grow their **NEW**. I therefore urge you not to overlook the financial benefits that you may derive from making an investment in higher education if you can and if it makes financial sense.

Education is an intangible asset! You can't see or touch it but it can work for you to increase your **NEW** smartly each and every day!

An important conversation to have with your fiancé or spouse is whether it makes sense for one or both of you to further your education. If a decision is reached to go ahead with further education for one or both of you, then the next conversation has to be about how to make this financial sacrifice fair for both of you in the event that there is a divorce in the future.

Higher education is not cheap and could demand a big sacrifice.

NOTES

YOUR NEW AND YOUR EDUCATION (AVERAGE LIFETIME EARNINGS)

High School Diploma — $1.3 mill

Some College — $1.55 million

Bachelor's Degree — $2.27 million

Master's — $2.67 million

Doctorate — $3.25 million

Professional Degree — $3.65 million

- **YOU** are the person that you can depend upon the most to generate cash inflows to increase your **NEW**.

- **YOU** have the potential to generate more money for your **NEW** than any investment that you can make.

- **YOU** should therefore consider cultivating yourself to the fullest extent possible via college, skill or trade so that you can maximize your inflows during your productive years.

- Education can provide you with an intangible asset that should increase your earnings, allowing you to save more and grow your **NEW** accordingly.

"The College Payoff" Georgetown University Center for Education and the Workforce. Anthony P. Carnevale — Stephen J. Rose — Ban Cheah Released: August 5, 2011

NOTES

SAVING

 CASH FLOWING INTO YOUR NEW SHOULD NOT FLOW IN AND RIGHT BACK OUT. YOU HAVE TO SAVE.

- Save, save, save!

- Cash is precious – it does not grow on trees!

- Learn our 3 C's: Champagne and Caviar today; Cat food tomorrow.

THINKING WITH A NEW MINDSET

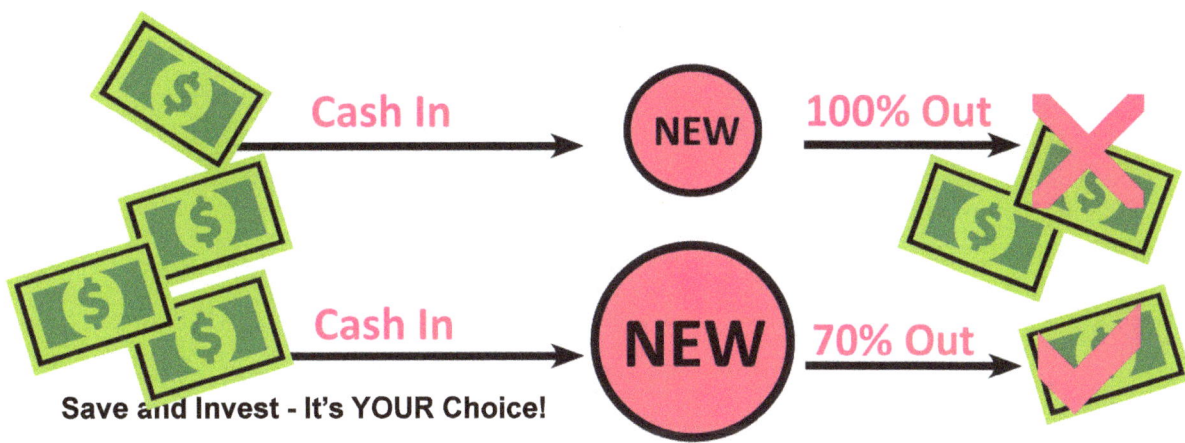

Cash In → NEW → 100% Out ✗

Cash In → NEW → 70% Out ✓

Save and Invest - It's YOUR Choice!

- Saving is a discipline and it is one that you can and **must** master.

- Come to grips with the fact that

"The Florida Keys Tooth Fairy" is not the solution to the growth of your NEW. YOU have to save so that YOU can then invest.

- It is best to develop a healthy attitude towards saving. Make it fun and make it work for you!

Florida Keys' Tooth Fairy

NOTES

SAVING STRATEGIES

- A good way to focus on saving is to establish a budget line item for each expenditure and each goal that you want to save for.

- Review budget items often and challenge the underlying vendors to see if you can spend less on particular items. Remember that when you spend less you indirectly save more.

- Never miss an opportunity to save either by producing more cash inflows or spending less.

- Consider having your savings systematically taken out of your checking account each month and moved to some type of savings account.

- The more years that you systematically save the more you will increase your NEW. Combine that with a solid investment plan and you should see your NEW increase.

FEED ME!

NOTES

INVESTING AND ACCUMULATING YOUR NEW

The reason for saving is ultimately so that you can enjoy the fun of investing and accumulating and reaching your financial goals

Later on in this book there is a focus on choosing the right financial professional to work with you on investing your savings.

Once you grasp the concept of the Magic of Compounding Interest and how you can make your savings work for **YOU** - you just may become a compulsive saver and investor!

EXAMPLE: If you save $5,500 at the beginning of each year and put it in a IRA that has diversified investments that are growing at 7% a year, over 20 years, the $110,000 you saved will more than have doubled. This is how you increase your **NEW.** You do it by saving and investing smartly.

THE MAGIC OF COMPOUND INTEREST AT WORK YOU YOU!

For 2019, the maximum you can contribute to all of your traditional and Roth IRAs is the smaller of: $6,000 ($7,000 if you're 50 or older), or your taxable compensation for the year

YEAR	TOTAL DEPOSITS	TOTAL INTEREST	IRA BALANCE
1	$5,500	$385	$5,885
5	$27,500	$6,343	$33,843
10	$55,000	$26,310	$81,310
15	$82,500	$65,384	$147,884
20	$110,000	$131,258	$241,258

You can calculate the future value of your own IRA: http://calcnexus.com/savings-calculator.php

The accumulation or the accumulating phase of your life is the years when you are growing your **NEW**. It is all about systematically saving and investing and holding on to what you have saved and invested. Accumulating **NEW** is a process and discipline that you should start as young as you can and continue until you reach a point in time when you no longer need to accumulate wealth.

The distribution phase of your life begins when you start to "spend down" your accumulated **NEW.** The distribution phase does not start at a specific age it starts when you have accumulated enough **NEW** whereby the income from your **NEW** investments can comfortably support your lifestyle. You can start the distribution phase at age 25 if it meets the criteria! You don't have to be 55 or 65!

NOTES

IMPORTANT CONCEPT: Whether you are single, about to be married, married or about to get divorced make sure that you keep your eye on what is inside of your **NEW** so that at all times **YOUR NEW** is positioned to keep accumulating. You do not want to be left in a position where you have to start taking distributions from your **NEW** before you have enough **NEW** to support your lifestyle for the long term. Talk to one or more professionals who can help you sort this out if you cannot do it for yourself.

An excellent way to Accumulate **NEW** is by setting goals and budgeting!

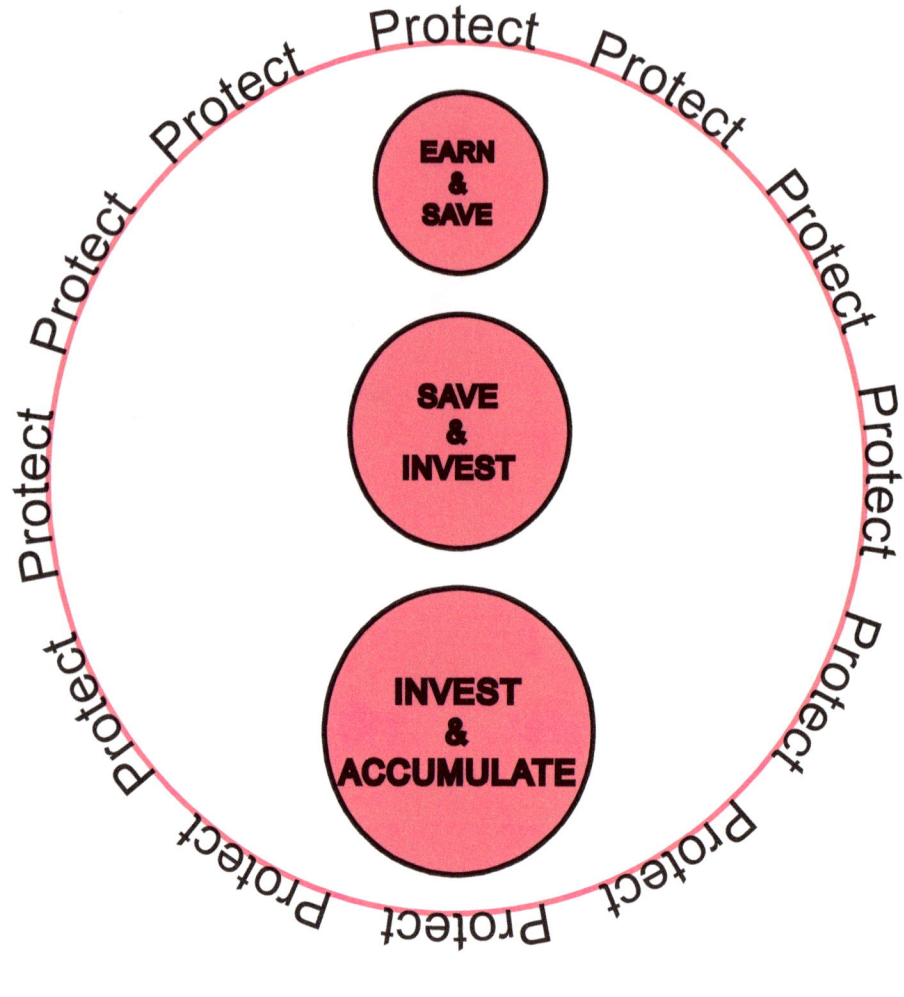

HAPPY RETIREMENT!

NOTES

THOUGHTS AND CONVERSATIONS FOR PROTECTING YOUR NEW

Question: Have you considered how fundamentally important earnings are to the accumulation and growth of your **NEW**?

Question: Do you understand the relationship between earning more and being able to save more?

Question: Have you had a serious conversation with your spouse or fiancé about your combined earning capacity and whether you all need to consider ways to improve this?

Question: Have you developed a systematic method of saving?

Question: Are you saving at least 15% of your annual earnings? If not, why not?

Question: Have you established a savings account specifically for emergencies?

Question: How many months will your emergency fund last?

Question: Have you considered ways to spend less and save more?

Question: Have you established an Individual Retirement Account or a Roth IRA account to help you save in a tax deferred environment?

Question: If your employer offers a 401K or similar retirement plan do you contribute the maximum to this plan each year. If not, why not?

Question: Have you talked to a financial advisor about helping you lay out a plan for saving and investing?

NEW FINANCIAL WISDOM

NEVER STOP PLANNING FINANCIALLY!

PLAN A: This is your plan if all goes well and you stay married.

PLAN B: This is your plan in case you face a divorce and have to support yourself and/or even your children.

REMEMBER THAT THERE ARE 24 MORE LETTERS IN THE ALPHABET THAT YOU CAN USE FOR EVEN MORE PLANS!

Learn the rules

and

KEEP PLANNING!

A NEW Focus on

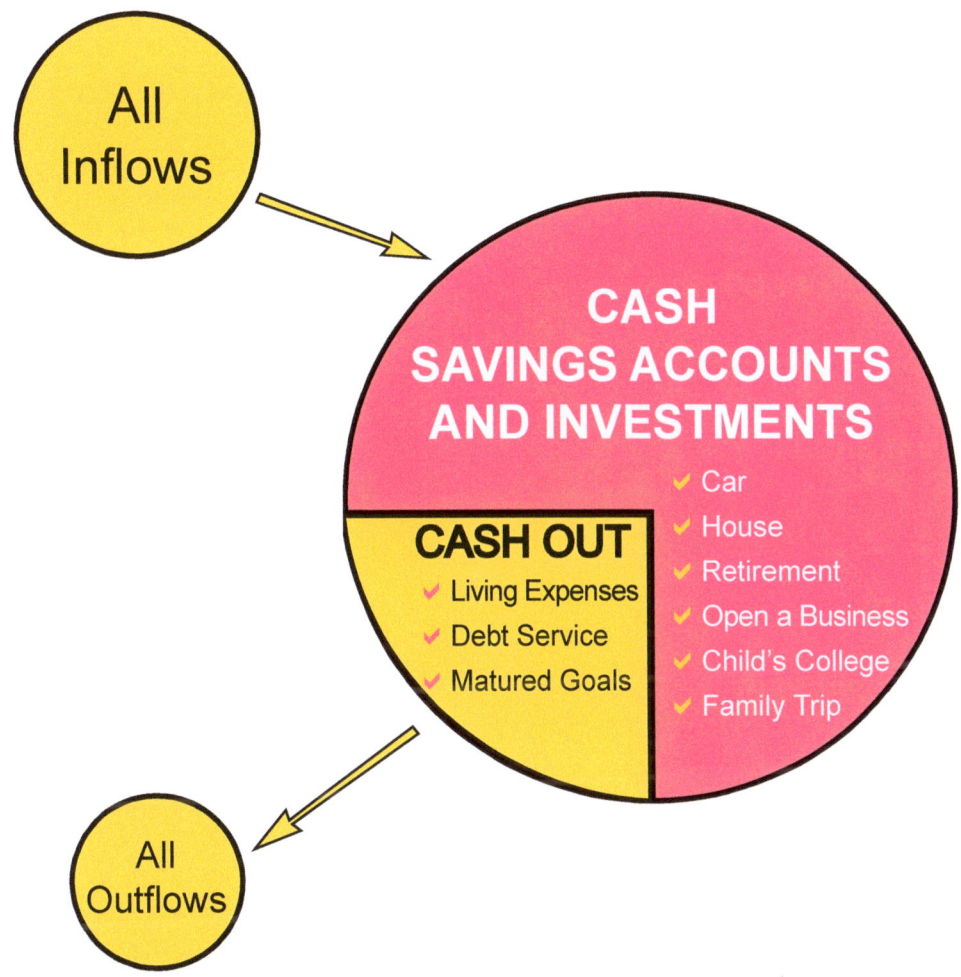

All Inflows

CASH
SAVINGS ACCOUNTS
AND INVESTMENTS

CASH OUT
- Living Expenses
- Debt Service
- Matured Goals

- Car
- House
- Retirement
- Open a Business
- Child's College
- Family Trip

All Outflows

THE GROWTH OF YOUR NEW IS ALL ABOUT SAVING FOR FUTURE
GOALS WHICH MOST IMPORTANTLY INCLUDES YOUR RETIREMENT

Setting Goals
and Budgeting

A NEW FOCUS ON SETTING GOALS AND BUDGETING

🐚 WHERE TO START

🐚 GOALS THAT YOU CANNOT OR SHOULD NOT FINANCE

🐚 GOALS THAT YOU CAN PARTIALLY FINANCE

🐚 THE SOURCES OF CASH INFLOWS THAT INCREASE YOUR NEW AND FUND YOUR GOALS

🐚 AGREE ON A BUDGET

🐚 WHY DO YOU NEED A BUDGET?

🐚 ADOPTING A NEW MINDSET!

🐚 WHAT FORMAT SHOULD YOU USE?

🐚 CHANGE

🐚 STAY INFORMED

🐚 BUDGETING WORKSHEET

IF YOU DON'T KNOW WHERE YOU ARE GOING YOU WON'T KNOW WHEN YOU GET THERE!

This FOCUS will help you to understand budgeting and the positive impact that a budget can have on helping you to materialize your financial goals.

A budget is not a set of handcuffs! A budget is an important tool for you to use in connection with building your NEW.

Budgeting is especially important when you are married because it is a great way to keep tabs on wasteful spending and also how YOUR half of the family NEW is growing!

Let's get started!

SETTING GOALS TOGETHER

A great FIRST financial goal should be to get rid of all short and intermediate term debt and then staying out of bad debt!

 **WHERE TO START**

- Saving to meet your goals is all about growing your **NEW**.

- The only reason for growing your **NEW** is to meet your goals.

- There are two types of financial goals:

  1 Cash Goals –the ones that need 100% cash.

  2 Goals that can be partially financed.

 **GOALS THAT YOU CANNOT OR SHOULD NOT FINANCE**

- Cash Reserve Fund for Emergencies

- Annual family vacation

- College Education Savings Fund (arguable)

- Special trip to Alaska or even a safari to Africa

- Retirement at age 65 or before

 **GOALS THAT YOU CAN PARTIALLY FINANCE**

- Buying a Car every 7 – 10 years

- Buying a Home or even a Larger Home

- Buying a Boat

- Buying a Vacation Home

NOTES

A NEW Focus on Setting Goals and Budgeting

❀ You may want to prepare a spreadsheet with the goals that you have so that you can compute how you are going to budget for each one.

❀ When you get through with your exercise, you may find that you can't afford everything that you think that you want. This is when you need to prioritize your goals.

❀ Divide goals between cash goals and the goals that you can partially finance.

❀ Recognize that, if you partially finance a goal, you still have to build the monthly payment for that goal into your budget. This may affect your ability to achieve other goals.

❀ Prioritize goals in order of importance and not necessarily in the order that you can achieve them.

Every couple has dreams. Put them down on paper and work them out in your budget.

Your budget is your **NEW** financial financial road map to make your dreams and goals come true!

EXAMPLE: Do not compromise your goals for retirement with your goal to have a very expensive car or boat that you really can't afford. Two kayaks may do just fine! JOKE!

❀ Fit monthly/annual payments into the budget or remove a goal for now if you can't afford it.

❀ You can lower the monthly savings amount for a goal by expanding the time frame to achieve it.

❀ Put the accumulation of cash for the goal on autopilot. Have the amount transferred automatically each month to your savings account.

❀ Check on your investments regularly to make sure that they are growing as planned.

Turn to case study #1 to see how setting goals without properly planning them out can be tragic, especially when debt financing is involved.

NOTES

THE SOURCES OF CASH INFLOWS THAT INCREASE YOUR NEW AND FUND YOUR GOALS

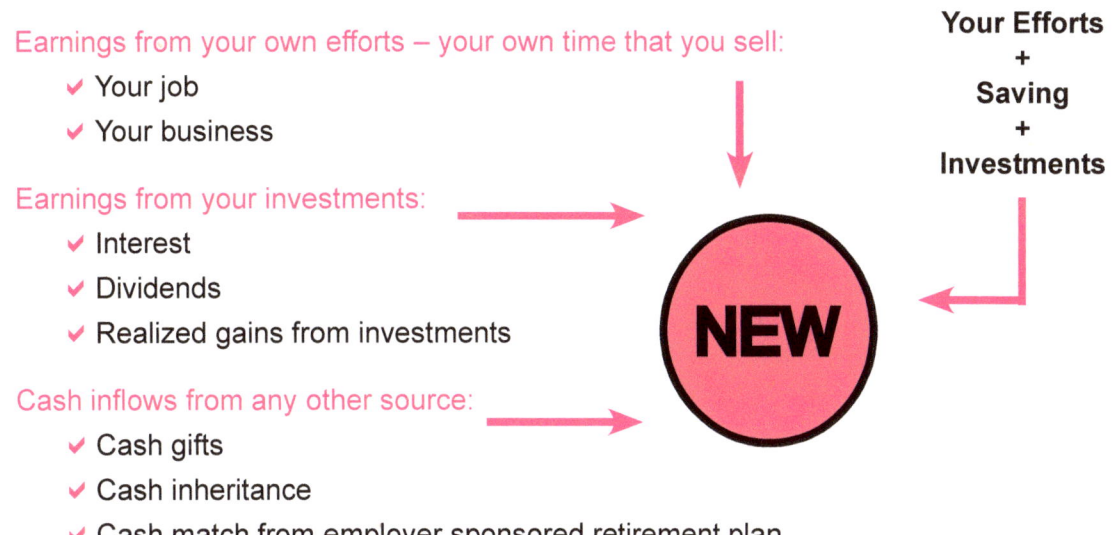

Earnings from your own efforts – your own time that you sell:

- ✔ Your job
- ✔ Your business

Earnings from your investments:

- ✔ Interest
- ✔ Dividends
- ✔ Realized gains from investments

Cash inflows from any other source:

- ✔ Cash gifts
- ✔ Cash inheritance
- ✔ Cash match from employer sponsored retirement plan
- ✔ Cash windfalls such as lottery ticket

Your Efforts
+
Saving
+
Investments

❋ Immediately, you realize that **YOU** are what it is all about. Inflows will come from **YOUR** job or business - your hard work.

❋ Internally generated income will then come from **YOUR** earnings that **YOU** have saved and which in turn have had the chance to appreciate in value and produce unearned dividends or interest.

❋ You cannot depend on externally generated inflows from any other source especially Prince Charming or inheriting from your parents. Remember, there is a possibility that you will get divorced and if you do, your **NEW** could be left in shambles if you are not prepared.

NOTES

BUDGETING

 ### AGREE ON A BUDGET

- It is important that you sit down and agree on a budget together.
- This is where compromising comes into play.
- Consider using a joint account for paying bills and individual accounts to hold an agreed-upon monthly "allowance" for each spouse.
- It is equally important that you stick to it and openly discuss your spending habits, for better or worse.

 ### WHY DO YOU NEED A BUDGET?

- You should REGULARLY analyze and know where your money goes not only on an annual basis but also on a monthly and quarterly basis.
- Budgets help you set realistic timetables for goals and major purchases.
- A budget forces you to come to grips with your spending habits and modify your spending behavior if necessary.

ADOPTING A NEW MINDSET!

- A budget isn't a set of handcuffs holding you back from spending your earnings.
- It is a tool to use as a road map to increase your NEW to meet your goals. Make budgeting your NEW best friend.
- Once you start working on your budget regularly you will find it liberating to know how much money you have coming in and where it is being spent. Knowing this will help you positively increase your NEW each month/year.

 ### WHAT FORMAT SHOULD YOU USE?

- There is no one set method for budgeting. Furthermore, although it needs to be thought through, it need not be complicated.
- Create one that reflects your spending and incorporates saving for things that are important to both of you.
- You can format your budget on an electronic spreadsheet or you can use an online version.
- Make it easy to review and update as circumstances change.

CHANGE

- Keep in mind that circumstances change including needs, resources, emergencies and goals. Inevitably you will need to adjust your spending plan as changes occur.
- If you have your budget set up on an excel spreadsheet you can make changes quickly.
- Annually go through your budget and look for ways to improve your NEW savings.

 ### STAY INFORMED

- One of you is likely to be a better manager of day-to-day expenses. It's okay to designate this person as the bill payer, but the other person should be involved and stay knowledgable of the family finances.

NOTES

A NEW Focus on Setting Goals and Budgeting

INFLOWS   -   OUTFLOWS

SALARY, TIPS $_____
DIVIDEND EARNINGS $_____
INTEREST ON ACCOUNTS, BONDS $_____
ALIMONY OR CHILD SUPPORT $_____
PENSION BENEFITS $_____
SOCIAL SECURITY BENEFITS $_____
GIFTS/MISC. $_____

TOTAL MONTHLY INFLOWS: $_____

ROUTINE LIVING EXPENSES
FEDERAL AND STATE TAXES $_____
RENT $_____
HOUSEHOLD REPAIRS $_____
AUTOMOBILE MAINTENANCE $_____
UTILITIES $_____
FOOD – GROCERIES $_____
FOOD - DINING OUT $_____
CLOTHING $_____
CHILD CARE $_____
INSURANCE: LIFE, HOME, AUTO $_____
MEDICAL EXPENSES $_____
ENTERTAINMENT $_____
TRAVEL AND GAS $_____
HOBBIES $_____
GIFTS $_____
CHARITABLE DONATIONS $_____

DEBT RELATED OUTFLOWS
AUTOMOBILE LOANS $_____
MORTGAGE $_____
OTHER $_____

TOTAL MONTHLY EXPENSES: $_____

TOTAL MONTHLY INCOME: $_____
LESS TOTAL MONTHLY EXPENSES: $_____
REMAINDER DISTRIBUTED TO SAVINGS $_____

SAVINGS FOR GOALS $_____
VACATION $_____
CAR $_____
HOUSE $_____
RETIREMENT $_____
CASH RESERVE FUND $_____
OTHER $_____

BALANCE YOU CAN ENJOY $_____

This sample budget is provided for illustrative purposes only. Be sure to customize your budget to suit your specific situation.

You can find many free Excel budget templates at: **http://office.microsoft. com/en-us/templates/**

Remember, A budget reflects cash inflows and outflows, not net income.

NOTES

THOUGHTS AND CONVERSATIONS for PROTECTING YOUR NEW

Question: Have you taken the time to have meaningful conversations with your fiancé or spouse about *your* dreams and goals?

Question: What are your 5 top financial goals in order of priority?

Question: Do you see a budget as a tool to help you get to where you want to go financially rather than seeing it as a set of handcuffs?

Question: Have you taken the time to separate your goals between financial and non-financial goals and then incorporate your financial goals in to a budget? If not, why not?

Question: Have you come up with a method or format for setting up your budget so that you can review and update it quickly?

Question: Have you considered using an electronic spreadsheet for your budget?

Question: How often do you plan to update your budget to make sure that you are staying on course?

A NEW Focus on

Managing Debt

A **NEW** FOCUS ON MANAGING DEBT

- UNDERSTANDING DEBT

- WHY DO PEOPLE USE DEBT?

- WHY FOCUS ON DEBT MANAGEMENT?

- MANAGEMENT OF DEBT PRINCIPAL

- MANAGEMENT OF DEBT INTEREST

- CREATING A NEW MINDSET SURROUNDING LIABILITIES/DEBT

- KEEP YOUR CREDIT CARDS IN CHECK

- DEBT DEATH SPIRAL

Using debt is a substitute for using cash and can destroy your **NEW**. Remember always that debt decreases your **NEW**.

This FOCUS will help you understand more about debt and provide you with useful strategies such as using a budget for minimizing the use of debt. You will also better understand why interest expense is so toxic to your **NEW**.

Let's get started!

UNDERSTANDING DEBT

Paying off debt and staying out of "bad debt" should be goal # 1 for many couples. Debt is toxic and very often causes severe marital distress. Whether one spouse has brought debt into the marriage, or credit card balances have soared during the marriage, you need to learn how to manage debt together.

* Debt Management can be broken down into several identifiable parts:

  1 The management of the principal repayment of your debt
  2 The management of the interest on your debt
  3 Your attitude and BEHAVIOR TOWARDS DEBT

WHY DO PEOPLE USE DEBT?

  1 Incurring a liability is a substitute for paying with cash.
  2 Convenience – credit cards allow us not to carry cash around.
  (If you pay off the balance monthly, and you have no annual charge, the convenience is free.)
  3 To make a purchase affordable by spreading payments over a period of time.
  4 Interest paid on some liabilities such as your home mortgage is tax deductible.

WHY FOCUS ON DEBT MANAGEMENT?

* Incurring debt has a negative impact on your NEW because it is a substitute for a cash outflow.

IMPORTANT CONCEPT: When you purchase an item using cash – that is the end of the transaction. When you finance the purchase of an item using debt – you immediately start to incur interest until the debt is paid off.

* Interest adds to the cost of a purchase and negatively and permanently impacts your NEW.

* The longer you finance a purchase or service the more interest you will pay and by definition the more negative impact the purchase will have on your NEW.

* To minimize the impact of interest on your NEW you have to look closely at the terms of financing and more importantly, you need to look closely at both the rate of interest being charged and also how the interest is being computed. NOTE: There is more than one way to compute interest. More on this later.

* If debt gets out of control, the interest will be a killer of your NEW.

* Getting a NEW MINDSET regarding your debt and managing your debt properly will help you minimize the negative impact of interest and debt on your NEW.

NOTES

TYPES OF DEBT

UNSECURED DEBT

* This is debt that is not secured by the lender, although they do have recourse to collect if not repaid.

* The lender has a higher risk of loss on repayment and therefore charges a higher rate of interest than on debt that is secured.

> **EXAMPLE:**
> CREDIT CARD
> SOME FAMILY
> LOANS

SECURED DEBT

* This is debt that is generally secured by the asset that was purchased with the debt. Because of this security the lender will usually charge a lower rate of interest than on loans that are not secured.

> **EXAMPLE:**
> MORTGAGE LOAN
> CAR LOAN
> BOAT LOAN

* In general, anytime that you can provide a lender with security for a loan, the risk of loss on the part of the lender is reduced and therefore the lender may agree to issue the debt at a lower rate of interest.

* This is why you can borrow against your HELOC (Home Equity Line of Credit) at a lower rate to pay off your credit cards. The HELOC is secured while the credit card debt is not secured.

NEW STRATEGY: It is possible to substitute collateral or even offer more collateral in an effort to get a lower rate of interest. This is a conversation that you should have with your banker or other loan company.

SHORT TERM DEBT

* Short term loans are usually repaid within one year or less.

* Examples of short term debt are:

> **EXAMPLE:**
> CREDIT CARDS
> TRADE ACCOUNTS

1 Trade accounts with vendors: monthly payment of balance in full. Interest may be charged on amounts unpaid after 30 days.

2 Credit Cards: Designed for the entire balance to be paid off each month. Not appropriate for financing larger purchases over time; a high interest rate is charged on unpaid balances and when this is not paid it is added to the unpaid balance.

NOTES

INTERMEDIATE TERM DEBT

- Intermediate term loans are generally repaid in 3 – 10 years and are usually used for financing purchases such as a car, boat, entertainment equipment, or furniture.

- Consumers need to be educated about these loans. They can be abusive in nature. Often there is an attractive first year or even first three years offer of no interest, after which the interest rates shoot through the roof.

- Interest on these loans can be calculated using either fixed-rate of interest terms or accelerated interest terms. While you pay the same total interest if you hold the loan for the full term, if you pay off an accelerated interest loan early, you may have higher interest costs than you would have with a fixed-rate of interest loan.

EXAMPLE: BANK OR DEALERSHIP LOANS

- More often than not the cheapest way to finance the purchase of an asset is via a bank loan with simple interest. The bank will typically offer a level monthly payment of principal and interest and also compute the interest based upon the unpaid principal balance.

Fixed-Rate of Interest Loan:

Principle: $ 10,000
Interest Rate: 10%
Anual Payment: $ 2,638
Total Interest Paid: $ 3,190

Year	Total Interest	Yearly Payment	Principal Payment	Loan Balance
1	$ 1,000	$ 2,638	$ 1,638	$ 8,362
2	$ 836	$ 2,638	$ 1,802	$ 6,560
3	$ 656	$ 2,638	$ 1,982	$ 4,578
4	$ 458	$ 2,638	$ 2,180	$ 2,398
5	$ 240	$ 2,638	$ 2,398	$ -
TOTAL:	$ 3,190	$ 13,190	$ 10,000	

Accelerated Interest Loan

Year	Total Interest	Yearly Payment	Principal Payment	Loan Balance
1	$ 1,063	$ 2,638	$ 1,575	$ 8,425
2	$ 851	$ 2,638	$ 1,787	$ 6,638
3	$ 638	$ 2,638	$ 2,000	$ 4,638
4	$ 425	$ 2,638	$ 2,213	$ 2,425
5	$ 213	$ 2,638	$ 2,425	$ -
TOTAL:	$ 3,190	$ 13,190	$ 10,000	

IMPORTANT CONCEPT: Vendors also make a profit on the terms of financing! If you are going to use an intermediate term type of debt you must do your homework to pick apart the interest and know how much it will really cost you. Any payment of interest negatively and permanently impacts your NEW. Don't get trapped into being sold a **monthly amount**. Do your homework.

NOTES

A NEW Focus on Managing Debt

 LONG TERM DEBT

* Long term debt is paid off over a period of 10 – 30+ years and is used to finance a large purchases such as a home.

* These loans are more often than not secured by an asset. Let's face it – who is going to lend you money for 30 years without underlying security?

* Types of long term debt are:

1 **Fixed rate mortgage:** Interest is fixed for the period of the loan. Amortization can be optional.

2 **Adjustable rate mortgage (ARM):** The interest rate is usually fixed for a period of years and is then adjusted using a formula based upon a widely recognized and published benchmark of current interest rates such as LIBOR. Amortization of principal can be optional.

3 **Fixed rate or adjustable mortgage with a balloon payment:** This is a popular mortgage with private lenders. Principal is repaid for a number of years, at the end of which, the balance is due.

> **EXAMPLE:**
> MORTGAGE ON
> REAL ESTATE

IMPORTANT **NEW** CONCEPT: You absolutely must shop interest rates for these loans because the interest directly impacts your **NEW** over the term of the loan. Interest rates can be negotiated and just because one bank or broker tells you that you won't find a lower rate don't believe them. Shop, Shop, Shop.

IMPORTANT **NEW** CONCEPT: Talk to your bank and a couple of mortgage lenders before you make an offer. Know your credit score so that you can give this to them. Get pre-qualified for a mortgage loan so that you can develop a financing strategy before you make the purchase. Keep reminding yourself about the negative impact that even one dollar of interest has on your **NEW**.

IMPORTANT **NEW** CONCEPT: ARMs are not necessarily a good deal unless you are predicting that interest rates will remain low. ARMs can come back to bite you if rates start going up and you cannot qualify for re-financing for one reason or another. Don't get yourself trapped. Even if you can re-finance, the re-financing costs are going to be a permanent hit on your **NEW**.

IMPORTANT **NEW** CONCEPT: If long term debt is properly structured at a fixed interest rate over a period of 20–30 years to purchase a home, you may be able to use debt to your advantage. Inflation will eat away at the purchasing power of the debt and payments, and you will eventually find yourself paying off the loan with cheap dollars. Sadly, this did not work to the homeowners' advantage during the recent Great Recession because prices plummeted and left homeowners "underwater".

Turn to case study #2 to see how incurring liabilities without title to the asset can cause BIG problems.

NOTES

🐚 MANAGEMENT OF DEBT PRINCIPAL

- Before you buy anything on credit, be it groceries, a TV set, jewelry, or even a home, the first question you need to ask is **NOT,** "Can I afford it?" but,

"HOW AM I GOING TO AFFORD TO REPAY THIS DEBT?"

- You must always have a plan for paying off any debt because of the negative impact of interest on your **NEW**. Remember, your financial game plan is to accumulate wealth, not give it away.

- **Check your budget** to evaluate whether you can afford to pay off a debt before you incur the debt. If you cannot readily find the answer there – Don't incur the liability until you have found the answer.

- Do not buy on credit based upon a promise such as a possible raise or an eventual inheritance from your parent. This is playing Russian roulette.

- **Always focus on the interest rates and repayment terms of the debt and not the amount of the payment.** Bad terms can lead to horrible results, such as negative amortization of the principal as interest rates go UP.

NEW TRAP: With consumer products such as an auto, boat or TV, always make sure that they are fully paid off by the time they are functionally depreciated. If not, you may find it impossible to sell the asset because the value will be less than the debt. (Upside down)

NEW TRAP: **Overspending** is a risk when credit is readily available. You have to make sure that your # 1 goal is not stepping into this trap.

NEW TRAP: Try to always borrow using "simple" interest rate terms and not accelerated interest rate terms. This way a larger percentage of your monthly payments will go toward repayment of principal.

NEW TRAP: Try to minimize the use of credit during financial emergencies. You do not know how long the emergency will last.

NOTES

MANAGEMENT OF DEBT INTEREST

● **Interest rates can be negotiated**, so always SHOP for the best rate before incurring debt. Always protect yourself from increases in interest expense.

IMPORTANT **NEW** CONCEPT: Since interest expense negatively and permanently decreases your **NEW** you need to **shop for the best interest rate on everything** before you buy. You also need to pay off your short and intermediate liabilities as quickly as you can so that you pay as little interest as possible.

NEW TRAP: One benefit of being able to use simple interest rates is that if you do decide to accelerate your principal payments you can benefit by doing this.

NEW TRAP: Do not assume that your "extra" principal payment will all be applied against the principal balance of your loan. Call the lender to make sure that all of your extra payments will be applied against your principal balance.

● One problem with interest is, unless you have a fixed rate loan (where the interest rate is fixed for the length of the loan), you cannot depend on the interest to stay at the same rate as when you incurred the debt. This is a potentially dangerous situation and another reason to pay off short and intermediate term debt as quickly as possible.

● The longer the term of the debt, the more interest you will pay. Since the payment of interest negatively and permanently impacts your **NEW**, try to pay down your debt as quickly as you can in order to get rid of paying interest. Many people double up on monthly payments, and this has a huge impact on reducing their debt; but don't do this unless your payments are being applied to your principal balance and in turn reducing your interest.

● Try to find a credit card that does not charge you interest as long as you pay off the balance in full within 30 days! Remember that, every time that you make a payment of interest, your **NEW** takes a direct hit.

NOTES

CREATING A NEW MINDSET SURROUNDING LIABILITIES/DEBT

- Since, incurring debt generally has a negative impact on **NEW** especially if the liability is incurred to purchase a consumable product/service or consumer depreciable goods. Before you purchase anything on credit, be sure to think through all of the implications.

- Analyze your spending habits. If you have a problem and cannot deal with it on your own – seek help.

- Learn to think through each purchase thoroughly in advance using your **NEW MINDSET** and make sure that you really need the item. Necessity vs. Desire!

KEEP YOUR CREDIT CARDS IN CHECK

✔ Come to grips with the fact that these are a convenience only and not a finance method for purchases over 30 days.

✔ Use one or two credit cards only. One for business and one for personal expenditures.

✔ Pay ALL credit cards off in full monthly and the day that you can not do this cut them up.

✔ Keeping separate cards allows you to track your individual spending habits; however, each spouse should have access to the credit card balance of the other spouse.

Turn to case study # 6 to see how problems escalate when credit card debt is out of control.

NEW STRATEGY: A credit card in your own name allows you to build up your own credit history. If you divorce your spouse or your spouse dies, it may be difficult or impossible for you to get a mortgage loan or credit card without your own credit history. A joint card in both names will not build up your personal credit history.

- Once you incur debt, try to throw as much money at it as you can afford monthly until it is gone.

NEW STRATEGY: Remind yourself that constantly incurring and accumulating debt has a negative impact on your **NEW** and can lead to a financial death spiral.

NOTES

A NEW Focus on Managing Debt

	YEAR 1	YEAR 2	YEAR 3	YEAR 4	YEAR 5
INCOME Only growing at 1.5% because of recession	$68,000.00	$69,020.00	$70,055.30	$71,106.13	$72,172.72
BUDGETED LIVING EXPENSES Includes income taxes, housing costs, food, clothing, entertainment etc. growing at 4% inflation	$50,000.00	$52,000.00	$54,080.00	$56,243.20	$58,492.93
SURPLUS AVAILABLE FOR SAVING OR INVESTMENT	$18,000.00	$17,020.00	$15,975.30	$14,862.93	$13,679.79
You buy a new boat and finance it over 10 years. Monthly payments of principal & interest are $275.	$3,300.00	$3,300.00	$3,300.00	$3,300.00	$3,300.00
You decide to buy a second home in Florida to go with the boat using an ARM. Monthly payments are $1,000 and increasing 3% annually for mortgage interest, taxes, insurance, etc. as they keep going up. Not to mention repairs and maintenance.	$12,000.00	$12,360.00	$12,730.80	$13,112.72	$13,506.11
SURPLUS FOR SAVINGS AND ALL OTHER EXPENSES	$2,700.00	$1,360.00	($55.50)	($1,549.79)	($3,126.31)

Problems:
1. Income not keeping up with Inflation
2. Living expenses going up 4% regardless of recession
3. Interest on mortgage not locked-in and rising
4. Any bad luck by year 3 and beyond will bankrupt/wipe you out

THOUGHTS AND CONVERSATIONS for PROTECTING YOUR NEW

Question: Have you had a conversation with your fiancé about debt that they will be bringing in to the marriage. Has this conversation included a plan for the repayment of this debt?

Question: Do you pay your credit cards off monthly and if not why not?

Question: Have you had a discussion with your fiancé about incurring debt and paying off credit cards monthly after you are married?

Question: Does your fiancé understand how toxic interest expense payments are to your NEW?

Question: Do you have a conversation with your budget before you buy high ticket items such a cars or furniture on credit?

Question: Do you use your budget to try to stay free of as much debt as possible?

Question: Do you try to save for high ticket items instead of buying them on credit?

Question: Before buying an item on installment do you discuss this with your bank to see if you can negotiate a better interest rate and terms?

Question: Do you have a goal of having your home fully paid for before you retire?

Question: Have you established a cash reserve fund so that if the unexpected happens, such as being laid off from your job, you do not have to incur debt to help you deal with this situation?

NEW FINANCIAL WISDOM

DO NOT SET YOURSELF UP TO BE A VICTIM

Risk is everywhere and risk is here to stay!

Learn to protect yourself financially at all times

and

STAY FINACIALLY FOCUSED!

A NEW Focus on

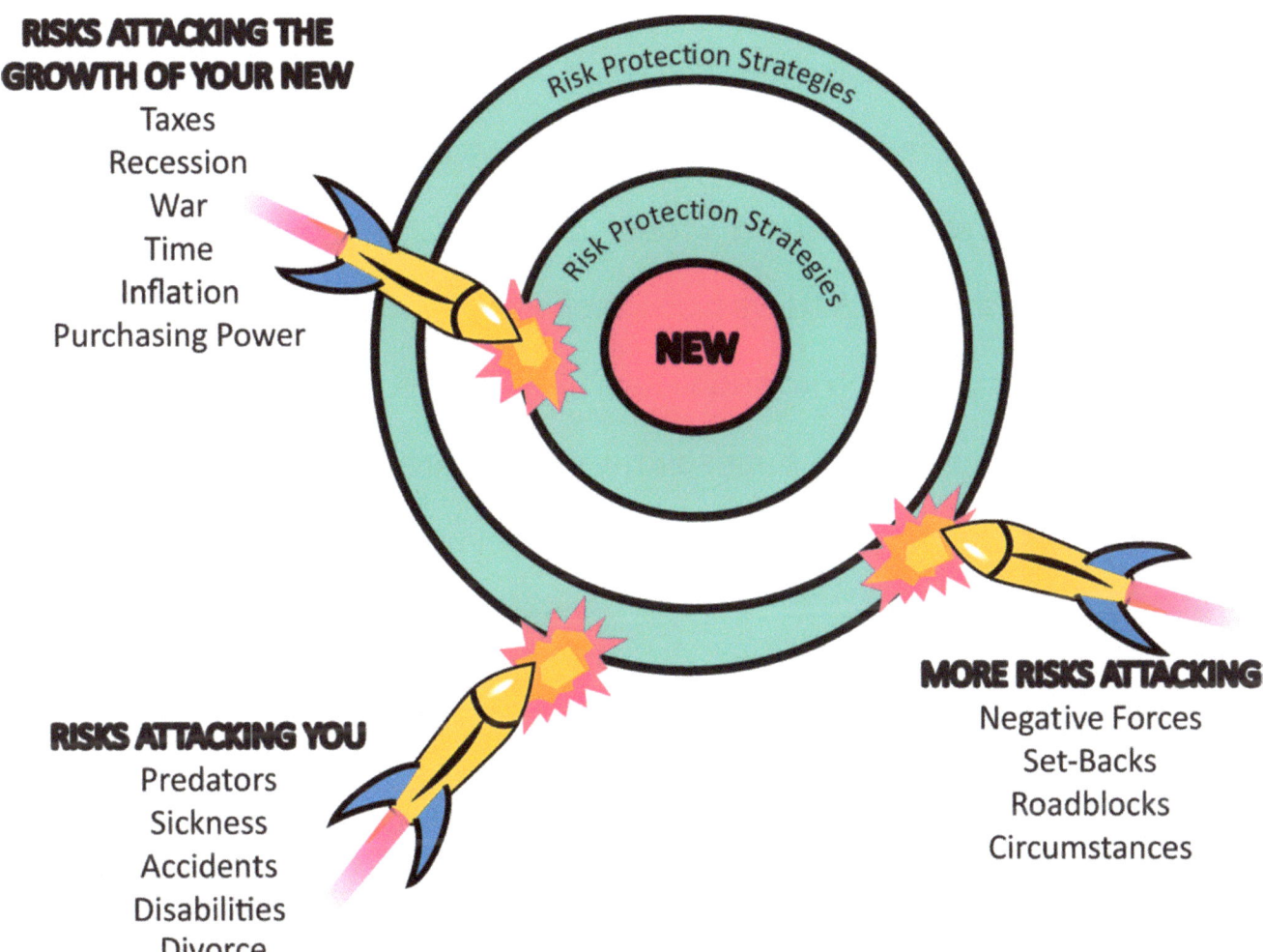

RISKS ATTACKING THE GROWTH OF YOUR NEW
Taxes
Recession
War
Time
Inflation
Purchasing Power

Risk Protection Strategies

Risk Protection Strategies

NEW

MORE RISKS ATTACKING
Negative Forces
Set-Backs
Roadblocks
Circumstances

RISKS ATTACKING YOU
Predators
Sickness
Accidents
Disabilities
Divorce

Protecting your NEW

A NEW FOCUS ON PROTECTING YOUR NEW

🐚 MANAGING RISK IS ALL ABOUT PROTECTING YOU AND PROTECTING YOUR NEW

🐚 PREPARE FOR THE UNEXPECTED WITH A CASH RESERVE FUND

🐚 HOW MUCH OF A CASH RESERVE FUND DO YOU NEED?

🐚 HOW DOES THE CASH RESERVE FUND RELATE TO YOUR NEW?

🐚 HOW CAN I START MY CASH RESERVE FUND?

🐚 INVESTMENTS APPROPRIATE FOR A CASH RESERVE FUND

🐚 REVIEW YOUR NEEDS ANNUALLY – TOGETHER!

🐚 LIFE INSURANCE – A MUST HAVE DISCUSSION

🐚 HEALTH INSURANCE – DO NOT GO NAKED!

🐚 DISABILITY INSURANCE – A MUST FOR THE BREADWINNER(S)

🐚 LONG-TERM CARE INSURANCE (LTC)

🐚 OTHER INSURANCE

🐚 REVIEWING INSURANCE AT LEAST ANNUALLY

This FOCUS is all about protecting and holding on to your NEW and reasons why you have to guard it at all times.

As long as you own NEW, someone will be making it their business to try to put your NEW in their pocket!

Let's get started!

RISK IS EVERYWHERE!

● Risk is…everywhere! Risk management requires you to identify, measure and assess your personal situation AND implement strategies that will minimize or mitigate the financial impact to your **NEW** if you and/or your family suffer a loss because of an unexpected event.

● While some events can happen that are bizarre in their nature, any number of losses such as sudden hospitalization for an unexpected illness, early death, loss of your job, or even an economic downturn can strike you down without warning and drain your family **NEW** dry unless you are prepared.

● Risks that you will be exposed to throughout your life will generally fall into one of three categories:

1   Those that cannot be managed

2   Those that are so remote from happening that they are not worth managing

3   Those that can be managed - These are what we will focus on.

NOTES

MANAGING RISK IS ALL ABOUT YOU AND PROTECTING YOUR NEW

- Risk management has to be planned in advance.

- Most of the time there will be a cost associated with putting a risk reducing strategy into place and that cost will immediately reduce your NEW. Don't get caught being "over insured". Always compare the cost of the protection over the years to the amount of the potential loss.

- Protecting YOU and **YOUR** NEW is the big picture! So, focus on YOU and YOUR NEW.

- If you understand that one of the foundations for increasing your NEW is through your own efforts at producing cash inflows, then it should be very clear that if something goes wrong with YOU, growing your NEW will fail.

- YOU will probably make more money during your lifetime than anyone will make for you and you should always remember that.

- **Consider this!** Protecting YOU and your cash inflow stream to your NEW is a key element to growing your NEW.

- Once the cash inflows are inside your NEW - protecting what is inside of your NEW becomes just as important. What is the sense in growing your NEW and then losing it?

- Protecting your NEW therefore encompasses protecting YOU, all of your investments and all of

your property from unnecessary risk of loss.

PREPARE FOR THE UNEXPECTED WITH A CASH RESERVE FUND

❀ What if you or your spouse lose your job or you suddenly find yoursef pregnant? If you and your spouse are caught unprepared, these types of situations can put a great deal of stress on your marriage and finances. As we discussed earlier, you cannot eliminate all risks, but you can prepare for them as a couple. Your budget should include a monthly allocation to build up your cash reserve fund for emergencies.

✔ A cash reserve fund is a combination of cash and/or credit that is available to you on demand to meet a short term and unexpected financial crisis such as the sudden loss of income from disability or loss of your job.

✔ In a financial crisis, you don't want to be forced to sell assets which may be temporarily depressed just because you need access to cash quickly.

✔ The cash reserve fund should never be used for normal recurring expenses such as payments for rent, insurance or vacations etc.

✔ The cash reserve fund should be composed of cash and liquid assets. In the face of a family financial crisis, your cash reserve fund can allow you to avoid using credit and going into debt.

✔ Look at your cash reserve fund as your "alternate airport" or even as a personal "treasure chest" in times of emergency.

🐚 HOW MUCH OF A CASH RESERVE FUND DO YOU NEED?

❀ This will vary from person to person, but usually 3-6 months of living expenses is a good starting point.

❀ An analysis to determine your personal monthly needs is an excellent place to start computing how much you actually need. Start with your budget to determine what you will need!

NOTES

HOW DOES THE CASH RESERVE FUND RELATE TO YOUR NEW?

* Savings will always increase your **NEW**.

* Spending in an emergency will decrease your **NEW**.

 HOW CAN I START MY CASH RESERVE FUND?

* If you don't already have a cash reserve fund, look to your budget to see WHERE you can cut back to start saving for one. Then, have the money systematically removed each month from your checking account and put into a cash reserve fund savings account. Check with your bank about multiple savings accounts.

* Keep the cash reserve funds separate from your regular bank account(s).

* See if you can reposition some of your existing assets, such as stocks or bonds to your reserve fund.

* Have a garage sale. Alternatively, use eBay to sell all of the stuff that you have hoarded and never use.

* Visit a local consignment shop and see if you can sell off some of your stuff there.

* Family heirlooms that have become dust collectors: Consider selling and getting rid of these on eBay.

* Sell gold and jewelry that you are no longer wearing.

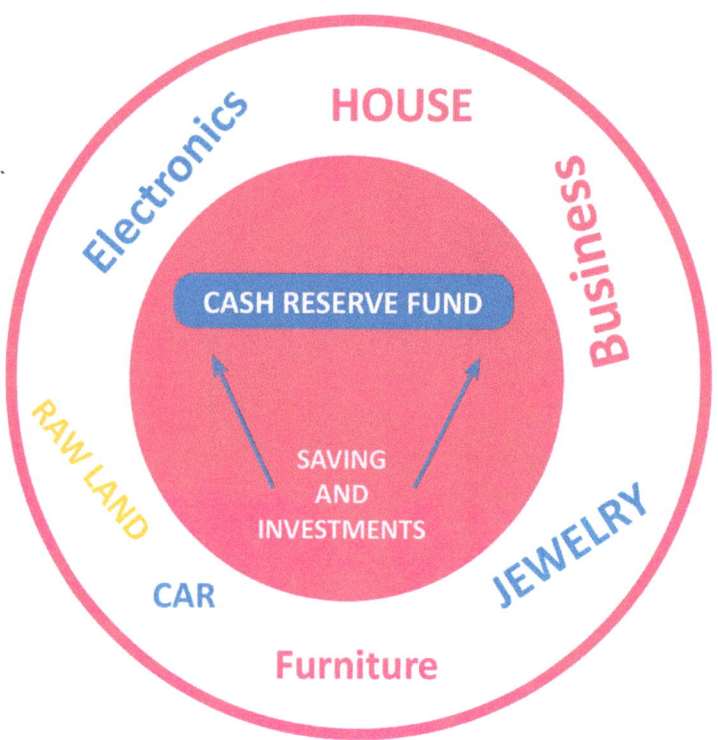

NOTES

INVESTMENTS APPROPRIATE FOR A CASH RESERVE FUND

- Liquidity is the key. However, the actual investments will be dictated by the amount that you need for your reserve fund. The more you need to have on hand, the more sophisticated the investments can be. For example, a relatively small cash reserve fund should only consist of cash, such as a checking or savings account, while a six figure fund may also include CDs, money markets, and treasuries.

REVIEW YOUR NEEDS ANNUALLY – TOGETHER!

- Your needs are apt to change from year to year. Review your cash reserve fund at least once a year and then make the appropriate adjustments.

- Please do not make the mistake of using your cash reserve fund for each and every emergency. An emergency is not a situation whereby you still have your day job but the TV broke down unexpectedly and you don't have the money to get it fixed immediately. Your cash reserve fund should only be used for real emergencies such as if you lose your job and you need these funds to support yourself and your family.

NOTES

HOW YOU CAN PROTECT YOURSELF AND YOUR NEW WITH INSURANCE

While we are focusing on risk, protection, and preparedness, we need to delve in to the importance that insurance plays in protecting you and your NEW. Will you be financially protected if you or your spouse becomes disabled or one of you dies unexpectedly? Will you be financially protected if your home burns down? Will you be financially protected if you crash your car or boat or if they are stolen?

LIFE INSURANCE – A MUST HAVE DISCUSSION

- You need life insurance to protect your family should one of you die prematurely

- The younger you are when you buy life insurance, the cheaper it will be, but the more payments you will make over the long run. This should not deter you from buying insurance.

- Your choices will be:

  - Permanent life insurance which is often referred to as whole life insurance
  - Temporary life insurance which is often referred to as term life insurance.

- You must be medically insurable before an insurance company will insure your life with permanent or temporary life insurance. So, do not delay in buying life insurance if there is a need!

- You can outlive your temporary insurance but permanent life insurance is in effect for as long as you pay premiums and are still alive.

- Permanent life insurance is not an investment but it does build up cash inside of the policy over the years as the premiums that you pay earn interest and these go towards building up a cash surrender value (CSV) inside of the policy.

- In the future if you no longer need insurance, you can cash in your permanent life insurance policy for the CSV or even roll it over, free of taxes, in to another insurance product such as an annuity, that could provide you with needed income. Unlike temporary or term insurance, with permanent insurance, you may get some money back if you stay alive and live to cash in the policy.

NEW BUILDING OPPORTUNITY: Do not cash in a permanent life insurance policy until you have had it valued. There is a market for people who want to buy the ownership of your permanent life insurance policy from you.

NOTES

* How much permanent or temporary insurance you will need varies. Here is a simple formula. Simply buy enough insurance to cover all of the family debts and the cost of dying and add to that amount the amount that you will need to invest to provide you with enough income to live comfortably without the income of your spouse. Remember that certain income such as social security income say "adios" when your partner dies. What are you going to replace this with?

* Talk to a licensed life insurance agent and they will help guide you.

* If you are married, you and your spouse can use a "last to die" policy if you are both insurable. This can reduce premiums and can be used to pay after death expenses such as estate taxes. However, there are several factors that need to be taken in to consideration before doing this. Think Divorce!

TAXATION OF LIFE INSURANCE POLICIES

* Premiums payments made by individuals to a life insurance company are not tax deductible by the owner of a life insurance policy.

* Death benefits paid to a beneficiary of a life insurance policy are not subject to federal income taxes when received and go directly to building their NEW.

* The dividends building up inside of a permanent life insurance policy are not taxable to the owner in the year that they are earned.

* If you do cash in a permanent life insurance policy with a cash surrender value (CSV) build up and if the CSV that you receive exceeds the premiums that you paid over the years, then the excess is taxable to you at ordinary income tax rates.

NEW TAX SAVING STRATEGY: The cash surrender value of a permanent life insurance policy can be rolled over free of federal income taxation into an annuity or to another insurance product under IRS code section 1035.

NOTES

DIVORCE AND LIFE INSURANCE

1 The cash surrender value of a life insurance policy is usually subject to division in a divorce.
2 The ownership of a life insurance policy can usually be transferred to another owner.

NEW PROTECTION STRATEGY: If you need life insurance as a potential substitute to cover child support or alimony in the event of the premature death of your ex-spouse, ask to become the owner of the policy that insures the life of your soon to be ex-spouse. This way you can guarantee that all premium payments are made on a timely basis and that the policy does not lapse.

NEW PROTECTION STRATEGY: If you are unable to take over the ownership of a life insurance policy in the event of a divorce, ask that you be designated as the irrevocable beneficiary of the policy until all spousal obligations have been met. This is not as strong a position as having ownership of the policy itself because your spouse could fail to pay the premiums on the policy and the policy could lapse. In this instance, you should insist that if your former spouse fails to make timely premiums that you are notified by the insurance company immediately that this has happened.

NEW PROTECTION STRATEGY: Another option is to take out a new policy on the life of your spouse, before the divorce is final, to cover the payments of child support or alimony in the event of the premature death of your spouse. If your spouse is not insurable this may present a new challenge for dealing with the risk of their premature death. This is a discussion for you to have with your divorce attorney. It may be possible for your attorney to attach other marital assets to guarantee these payments.

NEW PROTECTION STRATEGY: Do not get trapped in to having all of the life insurance proceeds from a former spouse go in to a trust for the minor child or children because you may not be able to use any part of it to help support yourself while you are raising the child.

 DEATH AND LIFE INSURANCE

* Insurance policies are paid to the beneficiary designated by the owner. Do not assume that because you got married that you will automatically become the designated beneficiary of your spouse's insurance policy. It does not work that way!

* Do not let someone else end up with the proceeds from the life insurance paid on the life of your dead spouse! You will need this money to get over your grief!

* It is a good idea to have the beneficiary designations changed on all life insurance policies before you get married. Beneficiary designation changes are very easy to implement and are NOT irrevocable.

* As previously mentioned, death benefits are not taxable when received by the beneficiary.

NOTES

HEALTH INSURANCE – DO NOT GO NAKED!

- No Brainer. You absolutely need it! It will negatively impact your **NEW** if you don't have it and you experience even a minor medical crisis!

- Health insurance can be offered by your employer or purchased by you.

- If you are covered under a Spouse or Significant Other's policy, and your employer is offering you insurance as well, compare and consider which one to choose and then try to get an alternative benefit for the one that you do not need.

- Often a primary insurance policy will not cover all of your medical expenses but you can supplement this with a secondary policy – or even a tertiary policy (think School Student Insurance, which may really come in handy when your dependent child suffers a sports injury).

DISABILITY INSURANCE – A MUST FOR THE BREADWINNER(S)

- Disability insurance offers you a percentage of your income should you be unable to work due to an injury or an illness.

- If you can buy it as part of a group policy, it can be very affordable and should not be overlooked.

- The cost will impact your **NEW**; but, if you become disabled, you will be very glad that you have it!

- The younger you are when you take out a disbaility policy, the cheaper the annual premiums will generally be.

LONG-TERM CARE INSURANCE (LTC)

- This provides for your needs should you require extended home or nursing home care.

- LTC is complicated, and policies have many moving parts; so educate yourself about them and use a competent insurance agent to help guide you through the maze of choices.

- The younger you are when you buy LTC, the cheaper the premiums will be however, you will make more payments in the long run.

- You need to pass a medical examination before you can buy a LTC policy. This is one good reason for purchasing LTC when you are young and healthy.

NOTES

OTHER INSURANCE

- Don't overlook the need for proper Homeowners coverage such as fire and theft, contents, windstorm, flood, automobile, boat and other personal tangible property.

REVIEWING INSURANCE AT LEAST ANNUALLY

- Your insurance needs should be reviewed annually. Babies are born, children leave the home, the breadwinner dies etc. Annual reviews can also result in savings via the cancellation of insurance that you no longer need or via using a company that is offering the same insurance for a lower premium.

STAY FOCUSED

The end game is to keep building up your NEW. Risk management plays a part in making this happen. Taxes, Divorce and Death can all deal a fatal blow to your NEW. Protect yourself by insuring losses that can potentially deal you and your NEW that fatal financial blow.

NOTES

THOUGHTS AND CONVERSATIONS for PROTECTING YOUR NEW

Question: Have you analyzed for yourself how important it is that you protect your **NEW** at all times and more importantly why you are protecting it?

Question: Has this FOCUS helped you better understand how to better protect your **NEW** from losses that are insurable?

Question: If you are married, how will you protect your **NEW** from the premature death of your spouse and the loss of that second household income?

Question: If you are married, how will you protect your **NEW** from the unexpected disability of either you or your spouse?

Question: Is it cost effective to insure your jewelry?

Question: Do you have health insurance coverage and if not why not?

Question: If you have a high deductible health insurance plan, are you using a HSA (Health Savings Account) to supplement this? If not, why not?

Question: Do you have adequate insurance to cover the loss of your home from fire or from a devastating flood or hurricane?

Question: What protection do you have if you crash your car and it has to be replaced?

Question: If your spouse dies do you have enough life insurance to 1) pay off any mortgages that you may have 2) Payoff all credit cards and other liabilities 3) Educate the children 4) Provide you with sufficient income to raise the family on your own?

NEW FINANCIAL WISDOM

THE THREE AMIGOS CAN HELP YOU!

Learn who they are and make them your friends

Use them to your advantage

Olé!

A NEW Focus on

Time, Inflation, and Purchasing Power

A **NEW** FOCUS ON TIME, INFLATION, AND PURCHASING POWER

- **TIME AS YOUR NEW FRIEND**

- **TIME AS YOUR NEW ENEMY**

- **WHAT IS INFLATION?**

- **HOW INFLATION EFFECTS YOUR NEW?**

- **IMPACT OF INFLATION ON YOUR NEW**

- **YOUR ULTIMATE "BIG PICTURE STRATEGY" TO DEAL WITH INFLATION**

> TIPP – TIME, INFLATION AND PURCHASING POWER will always be with us. This is why it is so important for you to understand these 3 amigos and how to make them your friend or how they can be your enemy!

Let's get started!

A NEW Focus on Time

When it comes to your financial future time cuts both ways. It can be your friend or it can be your enemy.

🐚 TIME AS YOUR NEW FRIEND

■ Time is your NEW friend when you systematically save and invest over a period of years.

■ There is wisdom in the old stock market strategy that states that "time in the market and not timing the market" that can make the difference. The concept here is that time smooths out the year to year ups and downs (volatility and risk) of the stock market.

■ Albert Einstein described **compound interest** as one of the greatest human discoveries! The concept of the "miracle of compound interest" is also a time related concept and refers to the potential for your money to grow faster as you earn interest on interest over time.

Now, let us look at the growth of $2,000:

Using a financial calculator you can project the growth of $2,000 invested today at 7.5% interest. In 50 years it will be worth close to $75,000. Even though you think that at 7.5% you will only earn $150.00 per year on the $2,000 and multiplying that by 50 = $7,500 – how does the investment of $2,000 end up being $74,379 in 50 years? The answer is the power of **compound interest** at work over time.

YEAR	TOTAL INTEREST	TOTAL AMOUNT
1	$150	$2,150
10	$2,122	$4,122
20	$6,498	$8,498
30	$15,510	$17,510
40	$34,088	$36,088
50	**$72,379**	**$74,379**

TIME is your friend when you start saving and investing early.

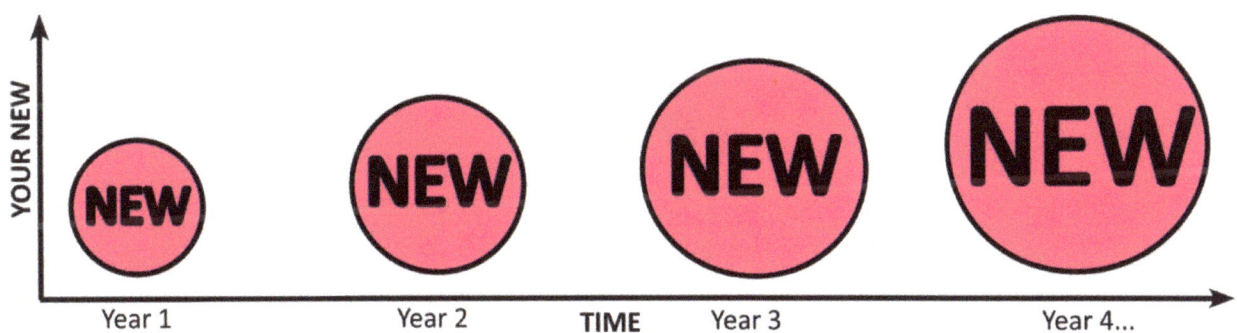

Harness the power of compound interest and your NEW will grow! Even a small investment can grow into a large amount of money over time.

NOTES

🐚 TIME AS YOUR NEW ENEMY

- Time is your **NEW** enemy when you develop financial paralysis and do nothing about growing your **NEW**. The longer you wait to start saving and investing the more difficult your wealth accumulation journey will be. You won't have time working in your favor and you will have to save more to catch up.

DELAYING SAVINGS:
Looking at it another way – the sooner you start saving the less you will have to save because of the magic of compound interest!

DELAYING THE IMPLEMENTATION OF PROTECTIVE RISK STRATEGIES TO PROTECT YOU AND YOUR NEW:
Time is your **NEW** enemy when you put off setting up protective strategies to protect you, your family, your property and your **NEW**. One stroke of bad luck can wipe you out completely and leave you in financial ruin. Everyday that you go without protection increases your odds of experiencing an unfortunate incident.

> **TIME, WE ALL HAVE IT – SOME PEOPLE USE IT WISELY AND OTHERS WASTE IT!**

TIME is your enemy when you live too long

Accumulation Phase: Your earning and saving creates growth in spite of inflation

Retirement Begins

Distribution Phase: You are now totally dependent on distributions from your **NEW** and feel the impact of inflation on purchasing power

NOTES

WHAT IS INFLATION?

RISING COST OF A US POSTAGE STAMP	
May 1978	$0.15
March 1981	$0.18
November 1981	$0.20
February 1985	$0.22
April 1988	$0.25
February 1991	$0.29
January 1995	$0.32
January 1999	$0.33
January 2001	$0.34
June 2002	$0.37
January 2006	$0.39
May 2007	$0.41
April 2011	$0.44
January 2012	$0.45
May 2015	$0.49
April 2016	$0.47

- Everyone has heard of inflation – it is on the news just about every day.

- Inflation is a rise in the general level of prices of goods and services in an economy **over time**. Simply put, inflation causes everything to get more expensive **over time**.

- Inflation is commonly measured by the Consumer Price Index (CPI) or the Cost of Living Index (COLI).

- This index is compiled monthly by the US Bureau of Labor Statistics and is easily available. The CPI tracks the changes in the prices of basic goods and services and therefore is a good measure of the changes in the rate of inflation. The CPI is used as a benchmark for making adjustments to a host of important things including adjustments to wages, Social Security payments and income tax brackets so that these costs stay in line with the purchasing power of the dollar.

- The **inflation rate** is the annualized percentage change in the CPI price index from year to year and over a period of time.

- One important fact you need to know about inflation is that it is persistent. We may have a couple of years of deflation but inflation keeps going on and on.

- We are not going to go into the details of WHAT causes inflation. Suffice to say that there are many schools of thought on this and the consensus is that there is not just one variable that causes inflation. There are many causes, such as when demand for goods are greater than the available supply, or when unemployment is low and workers can demand higher wages, or when there is too much money in the economy. Inflation can even be exported to and imported from other countries!

- The FEDERAL RESERVE and the CENTRAL BANKS in other countries implement monetary policies to keep inflation from getting out of hand. A small amount of inflation is considered healthy for the economy but too much is a big and very serious problem.

- Deflation is the opposite of inflation.

- Hyperinflation is basically inflation that has gotten completely out of control.

NOTES

🐚 HOW INFLATION AFFECTS YOUR NEW

- Inflation can be your friend or it can be your enemy – it cuts both ways and it is important for you to understand the impact of inflation on growing your NEW.

- The first aspect of inflation that you must understand is that you have absolutely no control over it and your best defense is to understand the ins and outs of inflation so that you can intelligently guard your NEW against the harmful effects of inflation.

- In the FOCUS ON TIME you saw the dramatic results of $2,000 invested over 50 years at 7.5%. Now we have to step back and understand the impact of inflation on this same investment that has grown over 50 years. Simply put, if your investment is earning 7.5% and inflation is 4%, then your rate of return after adjusting for inflation is only around 3.5%. Your actual inflation-adjusted rate of return will be 3.365%, but that is beyond the scope of this book! We will use 3.5% for simplicity.

END OF YEAR	TOTAL INTEREST	INVESTMENT TOTAL	PURCHASING POWER (Principal + Interest - Inflation)
1	$150	$2,150	$2,070
10	$2,122	$4,122	$ 2,821
20	$6,498	$8,498	$ 3,980
30	$15,510	$17,510	$ 5,614
40	$34,088	$36,088	$ 7,919
50	**$72,379**	**$74,379**	$ 11,170

Question: If inflation is growing at 4% and your CD is paying you 1.5% can you see that the purchasing power of your investment is actually going backwards by approximately 2.5% per year?

> "Inflation is when you pay fifteen dollars for the ten dollar haircut you used to get for five dollars when you had hair."
>
> - Sam Ewing, Author and Journalist

NOTES

INFLATION CAUSES THE COST OF EVERYTHING TO GO UP

FORCING

PURCHASING POWER OF THE DOLLAR TO GO DOWN.

If the annual rate of inflation is 6%, purchasing power goes down annually by 6%.

You have to outsmart INFLATION AND PURCHASING POWER.

Costing more

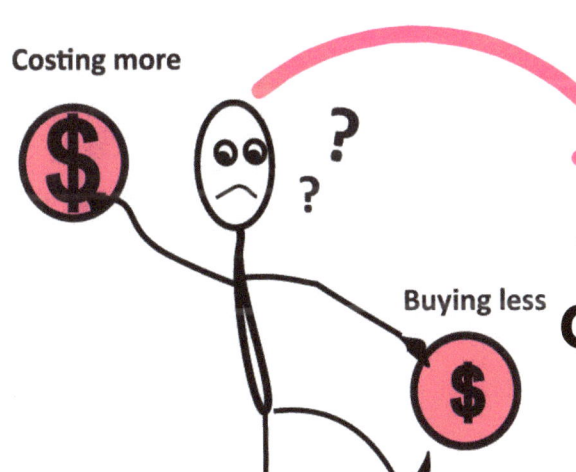

Buying less

ONLY SOLUTION: YOUR NEW HAS TO GROW FASTER THAN INFLATION.

NOTES

■ One of the key reasons for understanding the impact of inflation and loss of purchasing power on your **NEW** is to realize that the assets inside of your **NEW** are exposed to inflation and therefore, are open to the loss of purchasing power.

■ Your game plan for growing your **NEW** has to be that your **NEW** grows faster than inflation and the corresponding loss of purchasing power. Otherwise, you are going backwards.

IMPORTANT CONCEPT: Make sure that if you don't understand how to invest to protect your **NEW** that you seek help and find a financial advisor who can help you.

IMPACT OF INFLATION ON CASH

Inflation is especially harsh on cash that you own if it is sitting under your mattress.

■ If inflation is growing at 4%, then one of today's dollars will only buy the equivalent of 96 cents of goods and services next year. ($1.00 - $.04 = $.96) This is why it usually does not work to hoard your cash in order to avoid the risk of investing in the market.

■ Even savings accounts, money market accounts and CDs lose purchasing power when they are paying less than the rate of inflation.

■ Cash may be KING when you are trying to buy something at a bargain but every year that cash is idle it loses purchasing power equal to the rate of inflation.

■ Senior citizens with conservative portfolios that are heavily weighted toward safety are at a severe disadvantage when it comes to inflation. They tend to have more of their assets in savings accounts, money market accounts, CDs, bonds, and annuities for safety. Sadly, these assets feel the squeeze the most from inflation as the principal and income both generally lose purchasing power.

NOTES

THE IMPACT OF INFLATION ON YOUR RETIREMENT

INFLATION ON RETIREMENT PORTFOLIOS

Retirement is the time in your life when you are no longer working and are totally dependent on distributions from your **NEW** and other pensions such as social security.

■ The problem that many older people face is that as they age, they often want to reduce the volatility and risk of principal loss within their investment portfolios. It is very scary to have your **NEW** drop by 10%, 20%, or 30% when the stock market is tanking and distributions from your **NEW** investments are your main source of income!

■ To reduce portfolio volatility, retirees often allocate a larger percent of their assets to savings accounts, fixed income securities, and annuities. These all offer relatively low investment risk and provide stability to their portfolios.

■ Again, the problem is, while these savings accounts, fixed income securities, and annuities may be stable on paper, their value can be completely eaten away by inflation in the years ahead.

IMPORTANT CONCEPT: Just because the dollar amount of your portfolio is holding steady, this does not mean your **NEW** is not losing purchasing power to inflation.

Retire here!

✔ Smart saving
✔ Portfolio allocation designed to outpace inflation

✔ Goals: Retire with NO debt!

✔ Need distributions to be on "cruise control"
✔ Still need a strategy to help deal with inflation and loss of purchasing power

---

NOTES

YOUR ULTIMATE "BIG PICTURE" STRATEGY AND NEW MINDSET TO DEAL WITH INFLATION IN YOUR LIFE

- At all times make sure that you are aware of what is happening with inflation and how it is affecting your overall NEW. You need to make sure that your NEW is growing faster than inflation, or at least keeping up with it.

- This is easy to compute. The Bureau of Labor Statistics publishes the consumer price index monthly at: http://www.bls.gov. (Inflation is the annual percent change in the CPI)

- Keep an eye on the CPI and at the end of each year make sure that your NEW and related investments have kept up or outpaced the CPI for the year.

- When you are **SAVING** – make sure that your money is earning something to offset inflation. Discuss idle cash in your portfolio with an investment advisor.

- When you are **INVESTING** in the market – make sure that your diversification among asset classes includes asset classes such as stocks and real estate that can often trump the rate of inflation over time. Discuss this with your financial advisor.

- When you are **LENDING** money – **THINK LIKE A BANKER.** Be smart and make sure that the underlying interest rates that you are charging are adjusted each year for inflation.

INFLATION % + RISK PREMIUM % + YOUR RETURN = INTEREST RATE TO CHARGE

- When you are **BORROWING** money – borrow at a fixed rate – do not get trapped with an ARM unless it is for the short term and you are guaranteed that you can exchange the original note for a fixed rate mortgage later on without the hassle or cost of refinancing.

> **Always remember:**
> INFLATION NEVER STOPS!

NOTES

THOUGHTS AND CONVERSATIONS for PROTECTING YOUR NEW

Questions: Has this FOCUS helped you to understand TIPP (TIME, INFLATION AND PURCHASING POWER) and how these 3 amigos have an impact on the real growth of your **NEW**?

Question: Do you understand how to use Time, Inflation and Purchasing Power to be the friend, instead of the enemy, of your **NEW**?

Question: Are you monitoring your investments to make sure that they are growing faster than inflation?

Question: Do you understand why it is so important to start saving when you are young so that you have TIME and the power of compounding interest working for you?

Question: Do you understand why, when you are computing how much retirement savings you will need in the future, you must factor in to the computation the impact that inflation and the loss of purchasing power will have on your savings?

Question: Are **the** earnings from your salary or business keeping up with inflation? If not, why not?

Question: Do you understand why the growth of your earnings and investments must stay ahead of the annual rate of inflation?

NEW FINANCIAL WISDOM

DEAL YOURSELF THE WINNIG HAND!

If you quietly learn how to protect yourself financially, you can win.

Stay alert for potential issues and, as they arise, plan financial solutions and strategies to conquer them.

BE THE WINNER AND NOT THE VICTIM!

A NEW Focus on

Divorce Issues and Strategies

A **NEW** FOCUS ON DIVORCE ISSUES AND STRATEGIES

- WHAT ASSETS SHOULD YOU STRIVE TO KEEP IN A DIVORCE?

- MARITAL ESTATE AND MARITAL ASSETS

- VALUATION OF MARITAL ASSETS

- TYPES OF ASSETS

- DIVISION OF ASSETS AND DIVERSIFICATION

- MARITAL LIABILITIES AND DEBT

- TYPES OF DEBT

- DEBT CONSIDERATIONS

- ALIMONY

- CHILD SUPPORT

- SOCIAL SECURITY AND DIVORCE BASICS

- INCOME TAX, FILING STATUS, AND DIVORCE

- DIVORCE AND BANKRUPTCY

- DIVORCE AND YOUR ESTATE

"Instead of getting married again, I'm going to find a woman I don't like and just give her a house"
—*Ron Stewart*

In this FOCUS Bridal Financial Boot Camp brings the conversation full circle back to a more divorce issues and strategies. This FOCUS introduces concepts such as alimony, child support, social security, bankruptcy, income taxes, death and other useful information that you can keep in the back of your mind. Some of the information may seem repetitive but it is included again to provide reinforcement.

Let's get started!

A NEW Focus on Divorce Issues and Strategies

On the battlefield of divorce, you must protect what is rightfully yours and fight for the assets that will help you secure for yourself a bright financial future. Now that you have an idea of how to accumulate wealth it's now time to pay attention to the division of assets in the event of a divorce, and what to fight for.

NEW TIP: Planning is Key! Don't wait until you decide on getting a divorce to start trying to save and secure your financial future! You should have set up a plan before you said I DO! However, if you did not do any advanced planning, start planning as soon as you finish reading this book!

WHAT ASSETS SHOULD YOU STRIVE TO KEEP IN A DIVORCE?

In the FOCUS ON THE FINANCIAL FACE OF DIVORCE some, but not all, of the assets that may become a part of the marital estate were listed. The list is endless because it includes ALL assets owned by both spouses.

- Cash
- Real estate including the personal residence
- Notes Receivable from Family and Friends
- Employer Retirement Plans
- Individual Retirement Accounts
- Non-qualified Brokerage account
- Stocks, bonds, mutual funds
- Exchange traded funds, closed end funds
- Annuities
- Mortgages Receivable
- Family Business
- Partnership Interests
- Cash Surrender Value of Life Insurance
- Copyrights and trademarks
- Jewelry
- Boats
- All Vehicles
- Pets – Yes! Even the Pets!!!

NOTES

MARITAL ESTATE AND MARITAL ASSETS

THE MARITAL ESTATE CONSISTS OF BOTH THE MARITAL ASSETS AND MARITAL LIABILITIES that will be divided between the spouses in a in a divorce setting.

The determination of what is considered a "Marital Asset" depends on six main criteria:

1 Which State you legally reside in at the time of the divorce. State Law rules divorces! You either reside in a Community Property State or you reside in an Equitable Division State.

2 Whether you owned the asset before the marriage and whether you kept that pre-marriage asset separate during the marriage.

3 Whether the asset was gifted to you.

4 Whether you inherited the asset.

5 Whether you kept the gifted and/or inherited assets as separate assets during the marriage by not commingling them with marital assets.

6 Whether you entered in to prenuptial or postnuptial agreement governing the division of some or all of the separate and marital assets in the event of a divorce.

COMMUNITY PROPERTY STATES are Louisiana, Arizona, California, Texas, Washington, Idaho, Nevada, New Mexico and Wisconsin.

In Community property states, all assets acquired during the marriage are considered community property and are therefore marital assets. Marital Assets are owned equally by both spouses and are divided 50/50.

Negotiations may be possible.

Protect yourself by having meaningful financial conversations with your spouse about investments before they are made with marital cash. You may end up having to live with 50% of these assets!

NOTES

A NEW Focus on Divorce Issues and Strategies

EQUITABLE DIVISION STATES (also known as Common Law States) are all of the states that are not Community Property States.

Equitable Division States differ from Community Property States in that if your name appears on the title to an asset, you are considered the owner of that asset. However, your spouse does have the legal right to claim a fair and equitable portion of those assets in a divorce situation unless the asset meets the definition of a separate asset/property.

SEPARATE PROPERTY assets are assets that are titled in your name and are assets that were:

* Owned by you before marriage and kept separate after your marriage and not commingled with marital assets during the marriage.
* Gifted to you during your marriage and not commingled with marital assets during the marriage.
* Inherited by you during your marriage and not commingled with marital assets during the marriage.

In Equitable Division States just because you go buy and title an asset, such as a car, in your name during the marriage does not mean that your spouse does not have a legal right to place a claim on that asset. Furthermore, the equitable division of property in Equitable Division States may result in a 50/50 split up or it may not. Numerous factors are taken in to consideration in dividing the marital assets equitably.

* The length of the marriage
* The ages of the spouses
* The income of each spouse
* The future earning capacity of each spouse
* The standard of living established during the marriage
* Whether one spouse helped with the education of the other spouse
* The value that was provided by the spouse who stayed home and raised the children

NEW PROTECTION STRATEGY: Consider having a prenuptial agreement signed before you say I DO which specifies property that will not be subject to division in the event of a divorce.

NEW PROTECTION STRATEGY: Before you go commingling money received from a personal injury case that was settled during your marriage, discuss with your attorney whether you should keep this money in a separate bank account and if so how much. Usually, proceeds from a personal injury case is yours, except the proceeds that represent reimbursement for the loss of income. Don't get trapped with this!

NOTES

A NEW Focus on Divorce Issues and Strategies

NEW PROTECTION STRATEGY: Before marriage, talk to a divorce attorney about the disposition of the "future appreciation" in asset value of the assets that you own separately and that are titled solely in your name. The attorney may recommend that you enter into a prenuptial agreement that will clearly spell out that the appreciation in asset value will continue to be separate property in the event of a divorce. This is an especially important strategy for assets such as professional practices, businesses that are owned solely by one spouse before the marriage, and even real estate investments.

NEW PROTECTION STRATEGY: Property inherited or received by gift before or during a marriage are considered separate property unless these assets are commingled with assets that are marital assets.
Example: Wife inherits $ 250,000 in cash from her father's estate. Wife opens a bank account in her name only and deposits all of the cash in to this separate account. So far, so good. The cash is still separate property and if the couple gets a divorce, the cash will not become part of the marital estate. Wife will keep it all!

Example: Same situation except now the personal residence that they both own needs a new roof and the wife transfers $50,000 from the separate bank account to a joint bank account to fix the roof. Result is now fatal. The $50,000 in cash has now become commingled with a marital assets and is now part of the marital estate in a divorce! Bye Bye $50,000!

NEW PROTECTION STRATEGY: If your family gives you money to help you and your spouse buy a new home make sure that you get your husband to agree, in writing and witnessed, that the amount of their GIFT will never be considered a marital asset in the event that you and your husband get a divorce. It is these small attentions to detail that can add up and save your **NEW** in the event of divorce.

NEW PROTECTION STRATEGY: If you are gifted money or inherit money before or after your marriage and you maintain a separate bank account for that money DO NOT DEPOSIT any money earned during your marriage in to that separate account. Income earned during a marriage is a marital asset and by depositing income earned during the marriage in to the account you are "commingling" marital assets and non-marital assets. This can prove to be fatal in the future.

Example: Your mother gave you $50,000 as a gift when she sold her home. You put this money in a bank account solely in your name. You have a job and you and your spouse have decent salaries. You decide to start saving and begin to have automatic withdrawals from your paycheck deposited in to this separate bank account. BAD MISTAKE! You have now commingled a marital assets with a non marital asset. Better that you keep the proceeds from the gift separate from the savings from your pay check!

NOTES

THE MESSAGE IS CLEAR! Bridal financial Boot Camp cannot provide you with all of the Do's and Do Not strategies to use to protect your separate assets and marital asset rights during your marriage. What is important is that you make it YOUR business to become as educated, based upon the state that you live in, on what will be yours and not yours in the event of a divorce. Talk to an attorney prior to your marriage about property that you already own and/or may acquire in the future.

 VALUATION OF MARITAL ASSETS

Once the marital assets have been identified, the next order of business will be to have all of the marital assets valued. Division of these assets will be based upon their fair market value less any liabilities attached to the asset. Qualified appraisers and valuation analysts should be used. You do not want a jeweler to appraise your real estate!

NEW TIP: It is usually a good idea for the attorneys involved to agree in advance on the credentials of the appraiser and/or valuation analyst. Appraisals and/or valuations are expensive and subject to dispute, especially if there a small business involved. You don't want to be paying for this service twice!

Some of the assets such as a bank or joint brokerage accounts containing marketable securities can easily be valued and divided but other assets such as a professional business cannot be divided and may have to be exchanged for cash or the equity in another marital asset.

In extreme situations, the asset itself may be difficult if not impossible to value and/or so illiquid that neither party wants to accept it. In these cases, you may simply have to agree to put the asset up for sale and divide the proceeds when the asset is sold. You may find yourself kicking yourself for allowing your spouse to invest in this asset in the first place!

NOTES

INCOME PRODUCING ASSETS

One of the factors that you should keep an eye on while the division of assets is taking place is just where your future retirement income will be coming from. Even if you are still young when you are going through a divorce, do not overlook this! Always try to think ahead!

Example: what do you really know about that Oil and Gas Partnership that you own jointly and which is currently paying distributions of $200.00 per month? You may like the cash flow now but that partnership interest may or may not appreciate in the future. Furthermore, there may be a good chance that it will eventually go down in value in the future if it has less revenue to distribute to the partners! Do you really want to accept that asset versus accepting a larger percentage interest in the marketable securities that are owned jointly and which you understand?

Example: As mentioned before, the future income to be derived from $100,000 in a savings account is not the same as the income to be derived from $100,000 in a qualified individual retirement account! Having said this, there are pros and cons to accepting either one of these assets based on several factors such as your age and time horizon at the time of the divorce.

NEW SAVING TIP: A seasoned divorce attorney should be able to help you plan your future income and help you to identify and negotiate for assets that have a chance of appreciating and keeping up with inflation.

 ASSETS FREE OF DEBT

Debt carries its own risks. Suppose you lose your job after your divorce?

Try to take over assets that are free of any debt, even if it means liquidating other assets in order to accomplish this. An exception to this rule would be if your earned income allows you to comfortably afford to make the debt payments on the asset.

Remember that taking over an asset with an attached debt is riskier than taking over an asset that is free and clear of all debts. If you do take over an asset with debt attached, and are planning on paying down this debt with alimony payments from your ex-spouse rather than using income that you earn yourself, recognize that there is an additional RISK associated with doing it this way. You can't control what your ex-spouse will do in the future. Who knows, without your valuable guidance, they may become a deadbeat and quit their job!

NOTES

 APPRECIATING ASSETS

By now you should realize that you should try to take over assets that a   e versus ones that depreciate in value. Take the real estate over the boat or R.V. The real   ll probably be better for your **NEW** in the long run.

 TAX DEFERRED ASSETS

Because of the complexities and the many advantage and disadvantages of Employer Retirement Plans, Individual Retirement Accounts and Annuities, Bridal Financial Boot tCamp devotes an entire APPENDIX to these assets.

This does not mean that other assets owned in the marital estate are not as important as tax deferred assets. Bridal Financial Boot Camp treats these assets separately because of the many unique qualities that these assets share when it comes to Taxation, Divorce and Death.

 DIVISION OF ASSETS AND DIVERSIFICATION

If you are dividing a non-retirement brokerage account, insist that you get 50% of each security in the portfolio rather than taking 100% of some securities and 0% of others. This can only lead to potential trouble later.

Example: You jointly own 100 shares of RST stock and 100 shares of XYZ stock. Each stock sells for approximately $50 per share. If you take the RST stock and then the XYZ stock shoots through the ceiling. You won't feel that great! Better to take 50 share of each security for better diversification.

NOTES

MARITAL LIABILITIES AND DEBT

In a divorce, debts are also classified as marital debts or separate debts, similar to how assets are classified. Generally, it does not matter which spouse incurred the debt. Both spouses are generally held to be both responsible for the debt incurred during the marriage. You therefore need to understand the rights of creditors and how these rights affect you.

 SECURED DEBT

EXAMPLE: Auto loan, boat loan, home mortgage
Rights of Creditors: Lien holder or lender has the right to repossess the property in the event of a default.

 UNSECURED DEBT

EXAMPLE: Credit cards, loans from family or friends
Right of Creditors: Cannot repossess any specific property, but there are other remedies.
Either signor on a joint credit card can be held 100% responsible for the debt. It is not limited to 50%.

 TAX DEBT

EXAMPLE: An IRS audit results in taxes owed on a joint return from a year prior to the divorce.
Recourse: Each spouse is 100% liable to the IRS for the entire debt. (Ouch!). Protect yourself from this happening to you! Talk to your attorney before you agree to anything.

NOTES

DEBT CONSIDERATIONS - GENERAL RULES

1   State Law will governs who is responsible for each debt.

2   Community Property States will hold one spouse responsible for the debt of the other spouse because both spouses have equal rights in each other's assets, liabilities, income and expenses.

3   In Equitable Division states debt is usually allocated depending on who incurred the debt and what the proceeds were used for.

4   Usually, you are both responsible for any debt held in your joint names.

5   Once you have prepared an analysis of each asset along with their related debt, prepare a projected budget of your inflows and outflows to see if you will be financially able to take over any of the assets that you want along with their related debt.

   This analysis should guide you with respect to whether or not you should liquidate other assets to pay off debt or whether you can afford to take over certain assets along with their related debt.

6   Try to start your **NEW** single life with little or no debt obligation unless your income warrants your taking this risk.

STRATEGY: Consider filing "Married Filing Separately" while the war games are being played out. Later on, the returns can be reunited and filed as married filing jointly. This must be done within the statute of limitations.

NOTES

ALIMONY

Assets and liabilities aren't the only topics over which divorcing couples battle. All too often opposing lawyers turn alimony payments, child support, and retirement assets into war games. It is important to understand relevant issues, so you can proceed confidently and sensibly with a strong hand.

 WHAT IS ALIMONY?

Alimony is the periodic support payments by one spouse to another by a court-ordered Divorce Decree or Legal Separation.

- Alimony is governed by State Law.
- Alimony is often referred to as "maintenance."
- Alimony is based upon such factors as:
  - ✔ Need
  - ✔ Ability to pay
  - ✔ Prior lifestyle
  - ✔ Length of marriage
  - ✔ Age and Health
  - ✔ Contribution to Education

 TYPES OF ALIMONY?

- Rehabilitative – Short term, but not recognized by all states
- Permanent
- Modifiable – Can be increased or decreased.
- Non-modifiable
- A combination of the above

 WHEN DOES ALIMONY TERMINATE?

- By death
- By remarriage
- By agreement between the parties in advance

 GUARANTEEING ALIMONY PAYMENTS

- Insurance – Insurance – Insurance
- Life Insurance Trust
- Disability Insurance
- Annuities – Can provide a lump sum or monthly income for life.

 RECOURSE FOR COLLECTION OF UNPAID ALIMONY PAYMENTS

- Contempt of Court
- Wage garnishment
- Property liens may be possible in some states.
- Try not to get yourself in this position to begin with, because it costs money to chase down alimony.

NOTES

FEDERAL INCOME TAX RAMIFICATIONS RELATING TO ALIMONY

- There must be a written court order or separation agreement.
- If any amount is Child Support, that amount cannot be treated as alimony by the parties.
- Parties cannot file a joint return. Remember that filing status is determined on December 31st.
- Death terminates alimony.

ALIMONY RULES

Prior to 2019, the income tax rules and regulations surrounding the payment and receipt of alimony were complicated because the former spouse paying the alimony received a tax deduction for those payments whereas the spouse receiving the alimony had to include the alimony payments in their income tax return.

These rules sprouted an entire industry of strategies which, in turn, resulted in more IRS rules and regulations.

On January 1st, 2019, this all changed because alimony payments resulting in divorces that were finalized after December 31, 2018 are no longer deductible.

The old alimony rules still apply to anyone who was divorced prior to December 31, 2018.

Because alimony payments are no longer deductible, new planning strategies are now emerging. An example of this is the use of distributions from an IRA or 401k, via a QDRO, to fund and satisfy an alimony obligation. This and other strategies need to be carefully worked out by your attorney or CPA to make sure that they will be effective for YOU!

NOTES

WHAT ABOUT THE CHILDREN AND CHILD SUPPORT?

CHILD SUPPORT AND CUSTODY

- Child support is all about a parent's obligation to support a minor child. Minimum support includes providing for food, clothing and shelter. Each Resident State has minimum guidelines for child support.

- The custodial parent is the parent with whom the child lives.

- Joint (shared) custody occurs when the child lives with both parents. This is now common.

- Negotiations generally take place between the divorcing couple with respect to who will be the custodial parent and the amount of child support. Child support usually ends between ages of 18-21.

- If the child has special needs, it is possible for a judge to order continuous support for the child.

NEW SAVING STRATEGY: Child support payments are hard to collect. Try to secure these by attaching property belonging to your spouse.

CHILD TAX CREDIT

- A custodial parent may be eligible for an annual Child Tax Credit of up to $2,000 for a qualifying child. The credit may be refundable up to $1,400. IRS Publication 972 has more information about this credit and is available free, on line, at https://www.IRS.gov.

NOTES

HEAD OF HOUSEHOLD FILING STATUS

Head of Household filing status is a filing status that is available to parents who are single and maintain a household for a dependent. This is a filing status that is between filing Single and Married Filing Jointly. It is not that hard to qualify for this filing status.

 THE COVETED DEPENDENCY EXEMPTION

The question is just which one of the parents can claim the annual exemption for the child as a dependent on their federal income tax return. The dependency exemption usually goes to the parent who has physical custody of the child for the greater part of the year. This is regardless of how much money is provided by each parent. This dependency rule, stated above, does NOT usually sit well when one parent is paying a disproportional amount of the child support.

This custodial right can be waived by the custodial parent via the completion of IRS Form 8332 by the custodial parent whereby the custodial parent waives ONE YEAR AT A TIME his/her right to take the dependency exemption on his/her return and instead gives it to the non-custodial parent. The reason it must be done year by year is to enforce the rights of the custodial parent to receive payment of support for the child.

 CHOOSING AN APPROPRIATE FINANCIAL GUARDIAN FOR YOUR CHILDREN

Do not overlook this! Why? If you die and your minor children inherit your estate, the surviving parent will usually be appointed as both the custodial and financial guardian of the minor child, even if you are divorced. However, the surviving parent may be fiscally irresponsible. Your attorney can include language in your Will or a trust to make your mother or father or some other fiscally responsible adult the financial guardian of your minor children.

NOTES

SOCIAL SECURITY AND DIVORCE BASICS

This is where the woman usually takes a financial beating because, more often than not, the woman stays at home during the early child-raising years and does not pay in to the social security fund. Your Social Security benefit is based upon the amount that you paid in to the social security system. If your spouse worked while you stayed at home with the children, obviously, their benefit will more than likely end up being much larger than your benefit.

TAKE AWAY: The Social Security system does provide relief for this by allowing a spouse some benefit based upon the social security benefit of their spouse. A divorced spouse is also entitled to this benefit if the marriage lasted for at least 10 years.

One important financial topic that many women overlook in a divorce is the discrepancy in future Social Security payments between themselves and their ex-spouse. According to the Social Security Administration, 74% of unmarried Social Security recipients receive over half of their retirement income from Social Security! If you are in the midst of a divorce, Social Security needs to be part of the conversation.

NEW TAKE AWAY: Before you agree to stay at home and raise the kids, remember that you are not only giving up current earnings and future earnings potential, but you are also compromising your future Social Security benefit! This can have a major impact on your future retirement income. Talk about this before you make your move. You just may find that you will come out ahead in the long if those children go to day care. The 50% under your spouse's PIA may not be as much as your earnings record would provide if you worked and put the kids in daycare.

NEW STRATEGY: If you are unhappily married and you are considering divorce, think about how close you are to the ten-year mark, it might be worth putting up with that jerk for another year or two in order to get a better Social Security benefit! This of course is if your spouse's salary is more than yours!

NOTES

INCOME TAX, FILING STATUS, AND DIVORCE

- Once you are headed for the divorce court, you will be faced with decisions surrounding the filing of your individual tax returns. The best place to start is a discussion with your CPA or EXPERIENCED tax preparer.

- For Federal Income Tax purposes, Filing Status for the entire year is determined on the last day of your tax year, usually December 31st.

- When are you "unmarried"? When both your State and the Court say that you are. ("I divorce thee; I divorce thee; I divorce thee" does not go down well with the IRS.)

- For Federal Income Tax purposes, each filing status has its own set of rules and regulations as to who qualifies for each status. Fortunately, they are pretty easy to understand, but you should still discuss these options with your CPA.

✔ Single – Your divorce is final and your state and court say that you are unmarried.

✔ Head of Household – You are single and maintain a household for a dependent.

✔ Married – Legally Separated – You can usually qualify to file as single instead of Married Filing Separately. Make sure you know the rules relating to this.

✔ Married Filing Separately – Still considered married. A nasty tax bracket to end up in - the highest income tax rate that there is. Fortunately, if you maintain a home for a qualifying dependent, you may be able to claim Head of Household status.

✔ Married Filing Jointly – This is the lowest bracket. Everyone wants to use it. However, if you are headed for divorce, think twice.

MUST KNOW: Married Filing Separately carries the highest income tax rate. However, you can always amend two Married Filing Separately returns and turn them into one Married Filing Jointly Return prior to the time that the statute tolls allowing you to amend your return. Make sure that YOU get your fair share of the refund if you file separately and then amend to file jointly.

MUST KNOW: If you are asked to file a Married Filing Jointly return before you are divorced, be sure to have the other spouse indemnify you against any future taxes to be paid should the return be audited. Regardless, unless you are an innocent spouse, you will be responsible for 100% of the unpaid taxes if your former spouse does not make good on the indemnification.

NOTES

DIVORCE AND BANKRUPTCY

- Bankruptcy allows debts of the bankrupt individual to be wiped out so be very careful about accepting property settlement notes from ex-spouse unless they are collateralized by an asset because the note can be wiped out in the bankruptcy proceedings.

  - Alimony and Child Support are not discharged in bankruptcy. So, choose alimony over a property settlement note if you can and a property settlement over alimony!

  - Be sure to wipe out all unsecured joint debt prior to the divorce. Debt is toxic, and you don't want any part of it. You want to come out of the divorce debt free unless it works to your advantage to do otherwise.

DIVORCE AND YOUR ESTATE

- Typical estate documents consist of the following:

  - Last Will and Testament
  - Living Trust
  - Living Will
  - Health Care Surrogate
  - Durable Power of Attorney

"WHEN YOU ARE DEAD OR TRYING TO DIE YOU WILL STILL NEED SOME HELP FROM YOUR FRIENDS AND FAMILY ATTORNEY"

NOTES

A WILL

Your Last Will & Testament (Will) only kicks in and takes on a life of its own when you are dead. Basically, it deals with WHO will get your property and other things such as who will be the financial guardian of your minor children after you are dead. You name a Personal Representative in your Will to oversee the process for you. Usually, this is a member of the family. To breathe life in to your Will, the Personal Representative whom you have appointed hires an attorney who, in turn, takes your death certificate down to the local Judge as proof that you are indeed dead! This then starts a process known as Probate whereby the Court oversees the distribution of your property. Yes, even after you are dead you have to pay attorneys! After all of your debts have been paid and remaining assets distributed, the estate is considered "settled", and the Personal Representative is entitled to a fee for their services.

 A LIVING TRUST

There are many similarities and differences between a Will and a Living Trust. Importantly, a Living Trust can and does deal with "living" issues such as your standard of care when you are still alive but are unable or too frail to make these decisions for yourself. Instead of a Personal Representative, you appoint a Trustee in your Living Trust to make the decisions for you while you are still alive and after you are dead. A Living Trust survives your death and no one has to run down to the Court House with a death certificate for the Judge because a Living Trust does not need to be probated. Instead, it is the duty of the Trustee to distribute your assets in accordance with what you have set forth in your Living Trust.

Note that while working on your behalf, your Trustee is entitled to a fee for his/her services. It is always a good idea to have a Will even if you have a Living Trust as the Will can be worded to "pour over" in to your Living Trust any property that was not dealt with in your Living Trust. Ooops!

 A LIVING WILL

This is a legal instrument that has become increasingly important and evolved because of medical technology and innovations. It is mainly used by people who do not want to be kept alive artificially when the end is near but at the same time, they wish to continue to be treated humanely.

NOTES

A HEALTHCARE SURROGATE

While you are still alive, but in a situation whereby you are unable to make medical decisions for yourself, for whatever reason, you will need someone who can act as your Health Care Surrogate and make medical decision for you regarding such matters as "if and when to pull the plug"

 POWER OF ATTORNEY

This is a power that you give to a person whom you appoint to act as your legal representative if and when you do not have the capacity to handle legal matters for yourself. The person that you appoint to represent you in the Power of Attorney would use the Power to do things such as signing your federal income tax returns on your behalf while everyone is waiting for the Health Care Surrogate to sign off on "pulling the plug"! Oh yea! You still have to file a tax return while you lie brain dead in the hospital! The IRS shows no mercy!

- How to make changes to these documents:

  - ✔ A will can be changed by a codicil
  - ✔ A trust can be changed by an amendment
  - ✔ Other documents (are usually 1-2 pages)
    Have an attorney redraft and insert new names

- Make the changes as soon as you know that divorce is inevitable.

- Do not hesitate and postpone having your estate documents changed. Have the divorce attorney recommend an attorney who can do this for you timely. You really do not want your soon-to-be ex-spouse to have the ability to pull the plug on you. Do you?

TAKE AWAY: These are YOUR documents – they are all about what YOU want. You can change them whenever you want. Also, you do not need to discuss them with anyone other than your attorney.

- Where should you store them?

  - ✔ Keep them in a safe place where they can be easily accessed when needed.
  - ✔ Most law firms will keep a copy for you in their files.
  - ✔ Make sure you know where your mother, father, and your children are keeping their documents as well.

NOTES

THOUGHTS AND CONVERSATIONS for PROTECTING YOUR NEW

Question: Has this FOCUS opened your eyes to issues that you may have to face should your marriage end up in a divorce?

Question: Do you understand why it may be wise to enter in to a pre-nuptial or post-nuptial agreement?

Question: Do you understand how important it is for you to focus on your NEW
at all times and fight to protect it in the face of a divorce?

Question: Do you understand that not all assets have the same tax attributes and why it is so important to analyze the tax attributes of each asset that you accept in a divorce settlement?

Question: Do you understand why it is so important to look at the potential future appreciation of each asset that you accept in a divorce settlement?

Question: Do you understand why it is a good idea to "secure" agreed upon promises for future payments such as alimony or child support, via the use of insurance or other strategies such as a lien on available properties?

Question: Do you understand why it is important for you to try to avoid ending up with any debt as part of a divorce settlement unless you can comfortably afford to pay down that debt yourself?

Question: Do you understand why it is vital that you NEVER agree to be a co-signer, with your spouse, on a mortgage note UNLESS YOU ARE ALSO ON THE TITLE OF THE UNDERLYING PROPERTY?

Question: Do you understand why it is a good idea to have your estate documents updated as soon as you know that you will be filing for a divorce?

NEW FINANCIAL WISDOM

FUTURE SHOCK!

Remember that State Law governs.

A saving tip is to make sure that you have a decent understanding of the divorce laws in your State.

Never call your professionals and cry on their shoulders because they charge you by the minute.

Remember also, that it is not the attorney with the loudest bark that wins. It is the attorney who is the best poker player who wins the day for you.

A NEW Focus on

The Cost of Divorce

A **NEW** FOCUS ON THE COST OF DIVORCE

- **CHOOSING A DIVORCE ATTORNEY**

- **LEGAL FEES**

- **COURT COSTS**

- **OTHER DIVORCE RELATED COSTS**

- **DIVORCE MATHEMATICS**

- **PRIVATE JUDGING AND MEDIATION**

- **PRENUPTIAL AND POSTNUPTIAL AGREEMENTS**

- **DISAGREEMENTS BETWEEN DIFFERENT FINANCIAL PERSONALITY TYPES**

- **PRODUCTIVE FINANCIAL CONVERSATIONS**

- **SAMPLE PRE-MARRIAGE CONVERSATIONS**

So, how much does a divorce cost?

It is not only the cost of the attorney that hurts. It is also the other costs related to endless appraisals and court costs and other costs that can quickly add up. After a while, it seems as if the divorce has taken on a life of its own and become a money pit. You will learn more about these costs in this FOCUS.

Sorry – but do NOT try to do the divorce yourself on the internet! This is a very bad idea.

Let's get started!

CHOOSING A DIVORCE ATTORNEY

A good divorce attorney will be knowledgeable in:

1 **Family Law:** First and foremost, you want to choose an attorney with a specialty designation in Family Law in the state where you reside. Most states have a specialty designation in Family Law. If you have residences or other property in several states, more than one attorney may have to work on the case.

2 **Mediation and Negotiation:** This needs to be a top priority. You don't want someone who simply barks and threatens. You want someone who is trained to mediate and negotiate. If he or she is a good poker player, that is a definite plus.

3 **Accounting:** The attorney will have to deal with many accounting issues and needs to know how to add, subtract, multiply and divide!

4 **Basic tax laws:** Think property division, alimony, child support issues, interpretation of income tax returns, corporate and partnership returns, etc.

5 **Corporate Law:** Your attorney should be knowledgeable and familiar with corporate law, as issues pertaining to corporations and/or partnerships are common, especially if a family owned business is involved in your divorce.

6 **Child custody law:** Your attorney should be knowledgeable about child custody laws and be informed of any other personal aspects impacting your child or children.

7 **Real Estate Law:** If there is real estate involved in the divorce.

8 **Valuation basics:** You need an attorney who can look at an appraisal and recognize if it is flawed or otherwise lacking. This takes experience.

9 **Good listener:** Too often the attorney will become professionally hardened and view your divorce as nothing more than just another process. This can be frustrating to you if there are subtleties in your situation that you are trying to express.

NOTES

Finding an attorney who is not cynical and who really does view your divorce as a unique problem may be difficult. But there are experienced attorneys who have these qualities, and you will be able to find one. Do not be scared to ask questions so that you will understand the law in your jurisdiction and be able to envision and question the possible outcomes.

It is not the best pit bull that ultimately prevails but the best negotiator. Do not get pulled into talk like this: *"Before this is all over I am going to peel your spouse like a banana and leave him naked. He is going to be sorry that he was ever born."*

This is just talk. All it will do is deceive you into thinking that your attorney can get more for you than you are entitled to get. Ultimately, it will add needless time to the process and cost you precious dollars, which will ultimately come out of your pocket. It can also drag the divorce process on needlessly and add to the cost.

State Law governs divorces. In the end, the best negotiator and poker player will be the most efficient and cost effective machine to use.

The divorce process entails endless negotiations. If either party is stubborn and/or makes the process unreasonably difficult, then the attorneys representing both sides are the winners. They love it. And why not? It is YOU, the clients, who are creating the billable time.

You hire an attorney to protect YOUR interests because it is impossible for you to sort it all out yourself. However, you can do some homework and get yourself prepared before meeting with your attorney.

A spouse who is well prepared and has a firm grasp on the state laws involved and the divorce process itself has a better chance of coming out ahead, or at least not getting "taken to the cleaners."

HIRING AN ATTORNEY

● Before hiring an attorney, schedule an interview. You need to learn in advance:

- ✔ Hourly rate
- ✔ How often you will be billed
- ✔ How out-of-pocket costs for appraisals, mediation, etc. will be handled

- ✔ What type of retainer will be required
- ✔ Qualifications
- ✔ Experience as a divorce attorney
- ✔ References (if you can get them)

NOTES

LEGAL FEES

- You will probably NOT avoid legal fees for the divorce unless you are fool enough to try to do the divorce yourself.

- Divorce attorneys charge by the hour, but this is usually broken down into 10-minute intervals. A one-minute telephone conversation could cost you 1/6 of an hour of time.

- You probably will have to sign an engagement letter and pay a retainer fee for your attorney to get started.

- Do not hire the attorney until you are sure that you are comfortable with him or her. Get a copy of the engagement letter and take it home to read before signing.

- At the time of the divorce the Judge will order that the attorneys be paid, usually by both parties.

- After you have reached an agreement with the attorney who will represent you, it will be your duty to deliver as much information as you can. This should be well organized and scheduled, so that it is easy for the attorney to grasp. Do not have it in a shoe box as if you are going to your CPA. Have a list of assets, liabilities, incomes, expenses, names of children, and other important information.

- If you fight, the attorneys win. Make sure there is as little fighting as possible.

TAKE AWAY: Legal Fees paid for a divorce are usually not tax deductible. However advice relating to the tax consequences of your divorce or for securing income are deductible on your income tax return under Schedule A, Miscellaneous Deductions. Discuss this with your attorney up front so that the wording of the attorney's invoices breaks down items that are deductible on your tax return.

TAKE AWAY: Attorneys need lists of properties that are both individually and jointly owned along with any liabilities attached to these properties. Make sure that you have all of this information well organized and in the greatest detail possible.

IMPORTANT TIP: Many people end up finding that all of the family files have been removed from their home by the time that they realize they are heading towards a divorce. DON'T LET THAT HAPPEN TO YOU! You may consider keeping an extra set of tax return copies and other financial information somewhere safe and secure, outside of your home. Storing documents electronically may help.COURT COSTS
The problem with ending up with a contested divorce is not so much the court costs but the TIME and ANCILLARY costs that build up while trying to get in and out of Court. The Courts are jammed with cases and even a situation where you need a simple ruling from a judge can take months. Furthermore, since divorces are usually not fatal, court dates can often get bounced around in favor of emergency hearings.

> ### NOTES

- Some of the costs that can mount up include:

  - ✔ Depositions time and costs
  - ✔ Court Reporter costs
  - ✔ Investigative costs
  - ✔ Filing fee costs
  - ✔ The list goes on as the divorce takes on a life of its own

OTHER DIVORCE RELATED COSTS

- The cost of valuing businesses, real estate, jewelry and other personal property such as cars, boats, trailers, motor homes. The list is endless.

- If one spouse is cheating it may be necessary to hire a private detective!

- If one spouse is hiding money and not declaring all of their income, a Forensic Accountant may have to be hired to try to find that missing money!

- Books which conveniently went missing for a business may have to be reconstructed

- One thing that you can count on is that each time that a professional is hired to perform a non-routine service related to your divorce, you are probably going to be charged at their maximum hourly rate for their service. Unfortunately this is simply the way that it works!

DIVORCE MATHEMATICS

IF YOU CAN WORK THINGS OUT WITH COUNSELING AND MEDIATION	IF YOU CAN'T WORK THINGS OUT
$1 + 1 = 3$	$2 - 1 = 0$
Question: Where did the extra 1 come from? Answer: The magic of "Synergy"!	Question: Where did the extra 1 go to? Answer: Attorney fees and court related costs!

NOTES

PRIVATE JUDGING AND MEDIATION

HOT TIP: Working with a Private Judge is a new alternative to traditional divorce proceedings

- Think Judge Judy!

- The court system is so clogged up and costly that a new industry is springing up, consisting of retired judges who are prepared to work part time and privately judge cases.

- Both parties have to agree to the private judge and to be bound by the judge's ruling.

- Private judges can be hired to do mediation. This can be useful because a private judge, who has sat on the bench, can give you great advice on how another judge will likely rule on a case.

- The privilege of using a private judge may not be available in the state where you are getting a divorce or there may be limitations.

NOTES

PRENUPTIAL AND POSTNUPTIAL AGREEMENTS

Prenuptial agreement: A contract entered into prior to marriage or civil union.

Postnuptial agreement: A contract entered into after a couple is married.

⚫ Prenuptial agreements in all U.S. states are not allowed to regulate issues relating to child custody.

Content can vary widely, but commonly addressed issues are:
- ✔ Waiver of Maritial Rights
- ✔ Division of property in the event of divorce
- ✔ Spousal support in the event of divorce
- ✔ Penalties for adultery

Most jurisdictions require five elements to validate a prenuptial agreement:
1. It must be in writing.
2. It must be voluntarily signed.
3. It cannot be unreasonably excessive.
4. It must be executed by both parties (not their attorneys) and notarized.
5. Both parties must have full disclosure

⚫ State laws vary. You put yourself in peril if you do not work with an experienced attorney on these agreements. Each state is different and your attorney will know these differences.

Prenuptial and postnuptial agreements are great tools for protecting your prenuptial **NEW** and should NOT be regarded in a negative connotation.

The problem is that the last thing that a couple is thinking about before marriage is divorce!

Prenuptial agreements are especially useful for protecting your **NEW** if you own inherited property, a business or other separate property before entering the marriage. Do not take a chance!

Postnuptial agreements are a great way to formalize "financial promises" made by one spouse to save the marriage.

Just remember that if you don't enter into a prenuptial agreement the state, in which you are residing, has one written for you and you probably will hate it!

NOTES

THOUGHTS AND CONVERSATIONS for PROTECTING YOUR NEW

Question: If you are faced with a divorce, how do you plan to find a competent family law attorney to represent you?

Question: If you have a family member or a friend who has gone through a divorce have you considered talking to them about their experience and what they would have done differently?

Question: Do you understand that attorneys usually work on an hourly basis and not a fixed fee?

Question: Do you understand that your divorce attorney may recommend that you use other professionals to help with the divorce such as CPAs and Valuation Analysts?

Question: During your marriage have you made arrangements to have a copy of your joint income tax returns stored outside of your residence some place where you alone can access these documents physically or electronically if you need a copy?

Question: If you are married, have you also made arrangement to have other important documents stored outside of your residence so that these are easily accessible if you need a copy of them?

Question: Before meeting with an attorney, from a cost saving point of view, can you understand why it is a very good idea to have lists of important information containing relevant information about your marriage, your children, how each property is titled, your incomes, your expenses etc?

NEW FINANCIAL WISDOM

PEOPLE DON'T CHANGE!

What you see now is what you are going to get after you are married.

Don't sell yourself short.

YOU DESERVE THE BEST!

A NEW Focus on

Financial Personalities

A NEW FOCUS ON FINANCIAL PERSONALITIES

- **INTRODUCTION**

- **DIFFERENT ATTITUDES ABOUT SAVING - SPENDING - INVESTING - RISK**

- **DIFFERENT ATTITUDES AT DIFFERENT LIFE STAGES**

- **MORE INSIGHT ON SAVER TYPE PERSONALITIES**

- **MORE INSIGHTS ON SPENDER TYPE PERSONALITIES**

- **MORE ON RISK TAKERS AND INVESTOR TYPE PERSONALITIES**

Bridal Financial Boot Camp next brings in to FOCUS and analyzes different financial personalities and attempts to provide you with insight in to the different financial personalities that can work well with you and your future financial goals versus those personalities that will not.

Some financial personalities will simply keep putting bad dents in your finances even to the point of eventually totally destroying your marriage and your financial future if you are unable to harness these and bring them under control.

"Before you marry a person, you should just make them use a computer with slow internet service to see who they really are"
—*Attributed to Will Ferrell*

Let's get started!

A NEW Focus on Financial Personalities

 INTRODUCTION

Discovering one another's financial personalities is something that you should explore and try to sort out before you say I DO because this could present a serious obstacle to your being able to reach your financial goals and a secure financial future.

If you are already married, it may also be one of the secrets to understanding why you and your spouse are always at odds over money matters. With the proper insight and analysis, you just may be able to work out a compromise that can triumph.

It is also imperative to learn how to have constructive financial conversations with your fiancé or spouse! Sorting out financial issues early on can be very healthy for a relationship in the years ahead. Even in a mature marriage, especially in a bad economy, partners still need to discuss financial matters. In fact, learning how to discuss money can often save a struggling relationship.

Different salaries, spending habits, and attitudes about money are touchy topics for many couples. As a result, it's no surprise that money issues are the driving force in 90% of divorces.

If you cannot rectify wasteful spending habits and lack of financial discipline on the part of your fiancé or spouse you just may want to move on. Who wants to be a bag lady or bag man in their old age? Let's put it another way. You can't bury your head in the sand and hope that the tooth fairy is going to fly in with a solution and save the day! YOU must confront and deal with this problem and the sooner the better.

 DIFFERENT ATTITUDES ABOUT SAVING - SPENDING - INVESTING - RISK

Your fiancé or spouse may be a saver a spender or have a high risk personality. You, on the other hand, may have a totally different or opposite financial personality. Saving, spending and risk personalities range from conservative to aggressive and in between these two are shades of grey.

IMPORTANT CONCEPT: Make no mistake about it. You need to have conversations about attitudes towards saving, spending and investing before you say I DO. Why? Marriage does not change personalities. In fact, people are on their best behavior before marriage. So, how are you going to survive financially and build your NEW if your spouse is a spendthrift and and/or a risk taker and you find yourself starting out from scratch again every few years because of constant bad financial decisions made by your spouse? PROTECT YOURSELF! Pitch a Fit. Put your foot down! Consider getting out!

At the end of this FOCUS is help with pre marriage conversations and also help with financial conversations for couples who have already said I DO.

NOTES

DIFFERENT LIFE STAGES

Younger adults can afford to be more aggressive than older adults because Younger adults have a longer time horizon to recover from saving, spending and investing mistakes than older adults. Importantly, younger adults have many years ahead of them whereby they can still earn money and add to their NEW. Younger adults also have TIME on their side which can enable them to recover from rough economic cycles that have placed stress on their NEW.

Older adults, on the other hand, eventually come to the end of their earning capacity years and their ability to add to their NEW. This is when they have to place more and more reliance on their NEW investments to play the role that it was designed to play which is to produce the income needed to maintain their lifestyle during their "graying" years.

IMPORTANT POINT: Social Security was never designed to be the only source of retirement income for anyone and you do not want to wake up and find yourself in a situation where this is your only source of retirement income. No one is happy living on fumes!

Because of these age-related factors, and unless money is in plentiful supply, financial changes or adjustments are often necessary for older Adults.

WHY YOU ASK?

Well, for one thing, although the end may be near no one ever knows for sure the year, the month, the hour or the minute when their end will arrive and that is the problem in a nutshell!

No one knows exactly how much more money they will need to take them to the end whereby they can gracefully slide in to their grave with just 10 cents left to their name!

It is rumored that your insurance company knows the exact day that you will die but that is nothing more than hearsay…or is it? Regardless, they are not sharing this information with anyone!

Bottom line is that if a person has not grown their NEW enough they often have to resort to radical strategies to survive as they get older. One strategy is to cut back on their lifestyle to conserve their NEW so that it will last longer. Another strategy is to adopt a more conservative investment portfolio with less risk and volatility in order to preserve capital and hopefully make it last longer.

What happens if your spouse is not on board with these NEW strategies to conserve your wealth?

NOTES

SAVER TYPE PERSONALITIES

SAVER PERSONALITIES		
CONSERVATIVE	MODERATE OR BALANCED	AGGRESSIVE
❀ Saves but never enough ❀ May follow a budget	❀ Saves and loves budgets ❀ Meets goals	❀ Scrooge! ❀ Saves everything ❀ Fun very seldom allowed

Aggressive Savers may well end up with a nice big **NEW** if they invest their savings wisely. However, if they are too aggressive with their savings habits, they can be impossible to live with! Can you live with person who never wants to spend any money and who even takes senseless risks in order to save?

TRUE STORY: BAD CHOICE BOOMERANG

Your spouse dies and you believe that there is a nice big juicy insurance policy waiting to be cashed in so that you can live the rest of your days comfortably. Incidentally, you did not kill your spouse.

You soon find out that your spouse, who was an aggressive and compulsive saver, decided to cancel the life insurance policies in an effort to save on insurance premiums. Your spouse never discussed this decision with you for obvious reasons.

This type of behavior is not uncommon with aggressive savers and can be destructive. Be warned!

Conservative Savers are usually easy to live with because they are not Scrooges like their aggressive saver counterpart but they often do not have a solid plan for building their **NEW**. Conservative savers do save but usually never enough because it usually is not their priority and they may or may not want to discipline themselves enough to follow through with a budget. They simply go with the flow.

NEW SMART STRATEGY: If you really have to marry a conservative saver, do your homework and try to make sure that you find one who has a job whereby they will end up with some type of pension that will partially make up for their lack of saving. There is nothing wrong with putting your foot down, if you find yourself in this type of situation, and insisting that the family adopt a solid savings plan and budget.

Balanced and Moderate Savers are the ideal. They usually have a detailed budget and have a plan for saving every month for every goal that you all have agreed upon. AND, they are not always nerds!

NOTES

MORE INSIGHTS ON SPENDER TYPE PERSONALITIES

SPENDING PERSONALITIES		
CONSERVATIVE	MODERATE OR BALANCED	AGGRESSIVE
• Scrooge! • Does not like to spend • Fun very seldom allowed	• Spends based upon budget	• High lifestyle • Spends everything • Borrows to spend • Hates budgets

Aggressive spenders usually end up with little or no NEW. They live beyond their means and if they don't have the money to buy something they want they simply borrow the money from whatever source they can find and with this reckless spending they keep putting big dents in to your hard saved NEW.

Aggressive spenders consider budgets a nuisance and never have one. Aggressive spenders are usually "Bananas" and you can't change them! You will learn more about Banana people later on in this book.

SANITY CHECK: Why put yourself in a situation whereby one day you find out that even if you decide to divorce your spouse, because of their excessive and wasteful spending habits, you will be inheriting half of the marital debt and will have to spend years digging yourself out of this or even going in to bankruptcy to resolve this miserable situation.

Find out about these excessive spending habits before you say I DO.

Excessive spending and borrowing seldom have a happy NEW ending!

Conservative spenders are Scrooges! They never want to spend money on anything. They are almost identical twins to the Aggressive Saver personality! They will, on the other hand, possibly end up with a decent size NEW if they can bring themselves to invest wisely. Can you live with a personality that never wants to spend money on anything and you are forced to feel like a bag lady or man all of your adult life?

Moderate and Balanced spenders will usually end up with a decent sized NEW. Balanced and moderate spenders will always ask questions like "do I really need this or do I simply desire it" before they go and buy anything. These people always do their homework and check their budget before jumping in to any type of debt.

NOTES

MORE ON RISK TAKERS AND INVESTOR TYPE PERSONALITIES

RISK PERSONALITIES		
CONSERVATIVE	MODERATE OR BALANCED	AGGRESSIVE
❈ Takes no risks ❈ Less trusting ❈ Under-matress personality	❈ Weighs all risks ❈ Makes sound decisions	❈ Is a risk taker ❈ Gambler ❈ Potential to lose everything ❈ No tomorrow attitude

Aggressive risk taker and investors are people who love "deals" and are prepared to take on a higher level of risk in return for higher returns on their investments. They are usually looking for MAXIMUM returns. Unfortunately, this works both ways. If they are too aggressive and take on too much risk they can end up losing most if not all of their capital and the family **NEW**.

Aggressive risk takers and investors also have the tendency to constantly want to buy in to "deals" that can behave like a roller coaster. These "deals" invariably end up with the loss of most, if not all, of the invested capital. Aggressive risk takers have GAMBLER personalities.

"BIG PROBLEM"

You are probably going to go nowhere with your financial future if your spouse considers the stock market a giant slot machine and has decided to invest your retirement funds accordingly. This is the type of attitude that needs to be sorted out very early in marriage!

Conservative risk taker personalities would probably be happier keeping their money under their mattress or in a savings account or invested 100% in bonds or fixed income. With some education and/or professional help they may be able to change.

Conservative investors have a low risk tolerance and do not like volatility. They are always terrified about losing their hard earned **NEW**.

NOTES

Conservative risk takers also tend to live a very narrow life because they never want to take on risk even in their personal life. Normal things like travel may even stress them to the limit.
Again, as young adults get older it is not a bad idea to start becoming more conservative. This trait may serve them well later on in life.

Conservative risk taker personalities often have a difficult time moving their money from under their mattresses or bank account in to a brokerage account or even investing in alternative investment such as real estate that may offer the possibility of earning a greater return.

TRUE STORY: UNDER THE MATTRESS

I was once asked by an attorney to visit an elderly lady whom the attorney was concerned about.

When I entered the lady's house I immediately noticed that there were envelopes poking out from under her sofas and as I peeped in to her bedroom I could see them poking out from under her bed.

I decided to talk to the lady about all of the unopened envelopes and she told me that she was just fed up with all the junk mail that she was getting every day and had decided that the easiest way for her to deal with it was to stuff them under the furniture. Recognizing a red flag, I offered to help her and called my office for backup staff.

We pulled 7 large garbage bags of mail from under sofas and beds in the house and then opened all of her mail. Surprise! We found envelopes containing hundreds of shares of blue chip stock certificates. When I questioned the lady about this she told me that years ago she had closed her brokerage account because she was fed up with all of the statements that they kept sending her and she asked the broker to send her the physical stock certificates.

The story goes on. Initially, she put the stock certificates in a safety deposit box at the bank but then she went to the bank years ago and removed the certificates from her safety deposit box because she believed that they would be safer under her bed.

This is one example of an extreme conservative investment risk taker personality!
The story gets better. We also found uncashed checks that she had received and we found that predators had invaded her bank account and credit card account and were helping themselves each month to a nice income for themselves!

NOTES

DISAGREEMENTS BETWEEN DIFFERENT FINANCIAL PERSONALITY TYPES

ARGUMENTS ARE STILL INEVITABLE, BUT MAKE SURE THE FIGHTS ARE FAIR

- Learn to compromise but stand your ground if you have to.

EXAMPLE: Balancing the need to pay off debt with the desire for discretionary purchases.

- Allow time to cool off. Agree that it is all right for the discussion to resume later on. If you still can't start the conversation or constructively discuss your finances with a neutral third party, recognize that you have a problem and deal with it.

NEW SAVING STRATEGY: You may want to end up keeping your investments separate. However, this needs to be in the form of a written post nuptial agreement because in a divorce your spendthrift husband will be entitled to 50% of your hard saved **NEW** absent a written agreement. Bear in mind also that the sword cuts both ways in a divorce and if his **NEW** happens to be larger than yours, then you could be the loser.

FOOD FOR THOUGHT:

1 WHAT IS YOUR FINANCIAL PERSONALITY?

2 WHAT IS THE FINANCIAL PERSONALITY OF YOUR FIANCE OR SPOUSE?

STAY FOCUSED

Remember that the objective for saving and investing and protecting your **NEW** is to fund your financial goals and to end up with enough retirement income to support your lifestyle during your retirement years.

NOTES

MAKE FINANCIAL DECISIONS A PRIORITY

🐚 PRODUCTIVE FINANCIAL CONVERSATIONS

- Schedule regular meetings to talk about your finances together. Weekly, Monthly, Quarterly – whatever works best for you.

- Don't wait until there is a family financial crisis to have a meeting

- Always start on a positive note.

- Be honest and open. You should discuss your annual income, debt, property, investments, and bank statements with one another. You can't plan for your financial future without knowing your starting point.

- Ideally, these conversations start long before you say "I Do."

🐚 SAMPLE CONVERSATION

Income:
- His income: Can we improve this?
- Her Income: Can we improve this?

Joint Investments:
- How are they doing? Are they on course?

401k Saving Account:
- Are we contributing the maximum amount we can to our 401k? How are the underlying investments doing?

Spending:
- His Credit Cards: All paid? If not, why not?
- Her Credit Cards: All paid? If not, why not?
- His allowance
- Her allowance

Goals:
- His Goals
- Her Goals
- Our Goals, college for the children

Retirement Goal:
- Are we on schedule? Are we saving according to our plan? Are our investments performing as expected?

Included at the end of this book is a guide to facilitate financial conversations before and during your marriage.

NOTES

THOUGHTS AND CONVERSATIONS for PROTECTING YOUR NEW

Question: Has this FOCUS helped you identify your financial personality? If so, what is your financial personality?

Question: Has this FOCUS helped you to identify the financial personality of your fiancé or spouse? Is this compatible with your financial personality?

Question: Does your fiancé often ask you to lend them money for some emergency? Should you consider this a red flag?

Question: Have you had a financial conversation with your fiancé to discuss your assets, liabilities, income and expenses?

Question: Based upon the above, does it appear that your fiancé has a high tolerance for risk?

Question: Have you had a discussion with your fiancé about using a budget?

Question: Have you had a discussion with your fiancé about incurring debt? What is the plan for paying off your debts?

Question: Do you realize that it is usually impossible to change a person's destructive financial personality even with years of professional help?

Question: Given the financial personality of your fiancé or spouse do you believe that you will be able to attain your future financial goals?

NEW FINANCIAL WISDOM

PREDATORS ARE EVERYWHERE

Predators all have one thing in common. They want to take your NEW and put it in their own pocket.

Predators come in to your life via your TV, your cell phone, your computer, your emails, the newspapers, text messages, twitter….. the list is endless.

LEARN TO CLOSE YOUR FINANCIAL BORDERS AND KEEP THEM SHUT!

A **NEW** Focus on

Financial Predators

A **NEW** FOCUS ON FINANCIAL PREDATORS

- WHERE FINANCIAL PREDATORS CAN ATTACK YOU AND YOUR NEW

- SHARK ATTACKS

- DOLPHIN PATTERNS

- WHAT IF YOUR HUSBAND IS THE PREDATOR?

- PIRANHA PACKS

> Financial Predators are everywhere and their game plan is always trying to steal your **NEW**.
>
> This FOCUS is designed to help you identify their techniques and clever ways and provide you with the tools that you need to put **YOU** in control when you find yourself being attacked by a predator.

Let's get started!

THERE ARE ONLY THREE ENTRY POINTS WHERE YOU ARE AT RISK AND FINANCIAL PREDATORS CAN ATTACK YOU AND YOUR **NEW**.

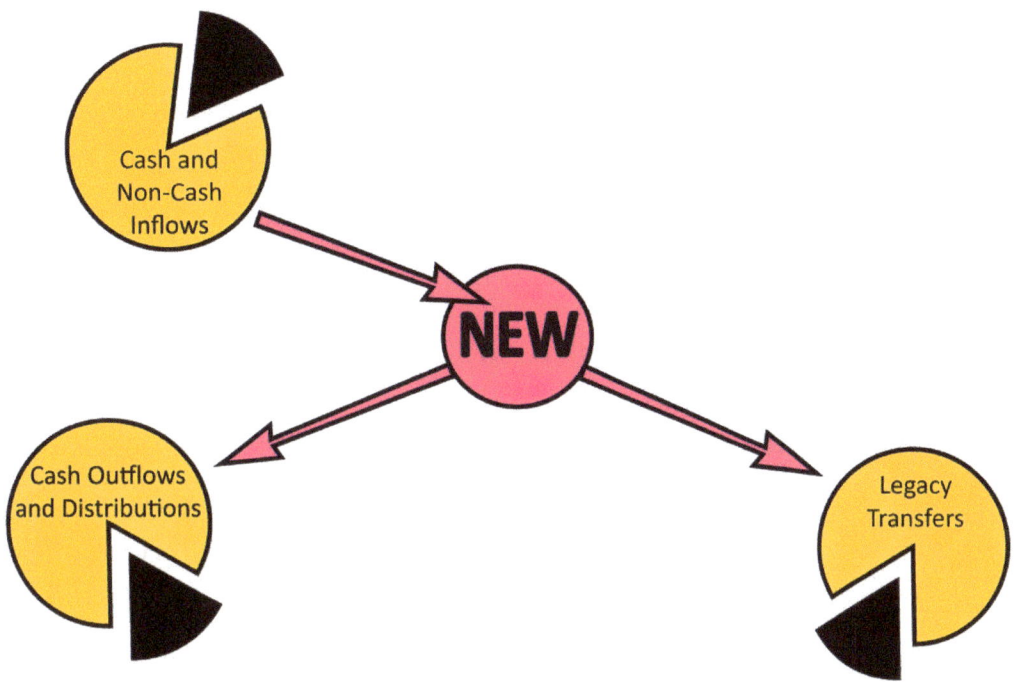

WE WILL TEACH YOU HOW TO SECURE YOUR BORDERS!

There are three types of Financial Predators; for purposes of Bridal Financial Boot Camp we are going to call them the sharks, dolphin, and piranhas.

NOTES

A NEW Focus on Financial Predators

 **SHARK ATTACKS!**

- The sharks are easy to spot because they usually approach you directly.

  - ✔ Internet phishes, scammers, and spammers
  - ✔ Identity thieves Organizations
  - ✔ Car salesmen

  - ✔ "Payday" lenders
  - ✔ Mutual Aid or Self-Help
  - ✔ On-line dating sites

- They are obvious, attack you first, AND have learned how to manipulate your emotional buttons.

- Current predatory tactics include the "grandchild with a bad phone connection" hitting up Gramps for cash. Facebook, YouTube, and other social media websites provide the source material for the predator to practice being your relative.

- Mutual Aid, self-help, and community service organizations such as Alcoholics and Narcotics Anonymous are experiencing an increase in predatory activity. Often a criminal will be required by the courts to attend one of these organizations. Once there, empathy between members, the "team" rapport, and the appearance of weakness by the predator trigger sympathy. The sharks will have direct knowledge of what they need to set you up for a financial hit because you told them.

- Online dating sites can be "fish in a barrel" for the sharks out there. Emotion and feeling lonely causes your built-in fight and flight instinct to fail. You have sought out this new relationship and put yourself out there. You have invited a Shark attack!

- There is no end to the schemes and tactics that sharks will employ. Best Practices against sharks:

1. Don't go swimming with sharks.
2. See above - DON'T GO SWIMMING WITH SHARKS!
3. Hang Up. Forget the word, "polite." Just Hang Up.
4. Tune Out. Turn your back on them and walk away.
5. Press the "delete" button on your computer.
6. Don't open email from unkown senders.
7. Let them know that your money is tied up in a trust and you can't get at the principal. If they try to drill deeper, act stupid and tell them that you really don't understand all of the ins and outs of the trust.

NOTES

DOLPHIN PATTERNS

Dolphins are cute. Dolphins are loved. Dolphins are nice to be around. Dolphins make everyone happy. While it is understood that dolphins are among the most sensitive and intelligent creatures in the world, it is because of this that they can choose when to be their most ruthless. And the ruthlessness is often directed at their own family members.

- Dolphins include your own family and loved ones:

  - ✔ Children
  - ✔ Siblings
  - ✔ Spouses
  - ✔ Partners in work or love
  - ✔ Co-workers
  - ✔ Friends

- Other predator dolphins include:

  - ✔ Unscrupulous Financial Advisors
  - ✔ Unscrupulous Registered Representatives
  - ✔ Unscrupulous Lawyers
  - ✔ Unscrupulous Insurance Brokers
  - ✔ Unscrupulous Bankers
  - ✔ Unscrupulous Mortgage Brokers or Lenders

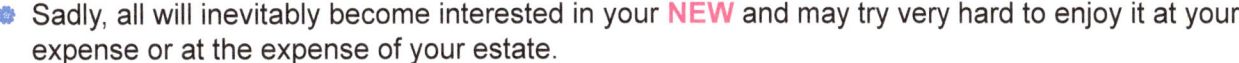

- Sadly, all will inevitably become interested in your **NEW** and may try very hard to enjoy it at your expense or at the expense of your estate.

- Some immediate family members such as children/grandchildren will play with your emotions, especially if they become your caregiver. They will not hesitate to eliminate other family members' interests by either getting you to put your property in their name or in joint names with them so that in the end they get it all for themselves. This is quite common.

- Professional predators may have the credentials and a clean and tidy appearance, but their intentions may not be in your best interest. Be skeptical even when you have been properly introduced.

- Getting a personal introduction to Mr. Madoff was a huge thing for some people!

- Often the simple act of being polite will place you in a position of weakness, labeling you as prey. Contrary to what your mom may have said, it really is okay to be rude sometimes. Try to use a strong handshake!

NOTES

PIRANHA PACKS

- Piranhas hunt and attack in packs. They have an understanding with a small group of their close buddies; and, when the time is right, they strike. They are so ruthless that in the process they may even take a chunk out of their buddy; but, once they have chomped into you, they will not let go.

- When financial predators join forces and are focused on their goal of working together to relieve you of your **NEW**, they are acting in collusion against you. You could end up as a financially dead fish.

  To protect your self against this type of attack requires that your advisors have separate and distinct areas of interest and control. In accounting and auditing, this is referred to as "segregation of duties."

- Here is another way that people can gang up against you, and it is more subtle because they rehearse their roles in advance.

EXAMPLE: You go to buy a new car...

1 You meet with the salesman to negotiate a price.

2 If he thinks that he is losing the battle, he will pass you to the manager, who will attack you from another angle.

3 If that manager is failing, you may be passed to yet another person in the agency.

4 Each person who you are passed to is trained to push yet another one of your emotional buttons until you cave in.

- These techniques are known as "selling tactics" and are quite legal unless the salesmen are lying to you about the product in order to induce you to buy.

- Use every tool in the tackle box provided in Bridal Financial Boot Camp to recognize and defeat predators so that you can grow and hold **on** to your NEW instead.

- Make sure that **YOU** will be the one to enjoy your **NEW** and not some predator.

Turn to case study #5 to learn how easily a predator can earn your trust and wreck havoc on your **NEW**.

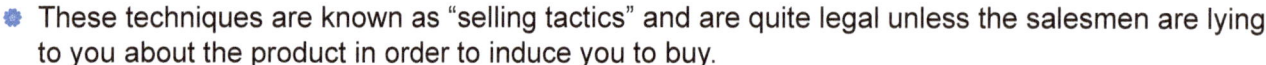

NOTES

WHAT IF YOUR FIANCE OR HUSBAND IS THE PREDATOR?

- ✔ He is always trying to get at your personal assets. Keep them separate!
- ✔ He is secretive about his business.
- ✔ He will always be "expecting money" from somewhere.

● Reading this book is your first proactive step! Understanding your **NEW**, your financial rights, and safeguards will help put you in a position to protect what is yours. Our predator tips and case studies will also help you spot suspicious behavior.

Speaking of "lover boy" predators, we want to address hiding money.

● It is easier than ever to trace hidden bank accounts, ATM withdrawals, and undisclosed business transactions online.

● If you firmly believe your spouse is hiding assets, work with a forensic accountant or family lawyer to discover the truth. Some types of snooping that you might be tempted to try yourself, like checking password protected accounts, can be illegal and inadmissible in court. Be careful!

● For more information on this subject, we recommend a great article from the Wall Street Journal that can be found here:

http://online.wsj.com/article/SB10001424052702304356604577337743171120240.html

NOTES

THOUGHTS AND CONVERSATIONS for PROTECTING YOUR NEW

Question: Did this FOCUS help you better understand the nature of financial predators and how to protect yourself and your **NEW** against them? What did you learn about financial predators?

Question: Do you understand the three entry points where financial predators can access and attack your **NEW**? Have you taken precautions to close these three entry points?

Question: In retrospect, have you ever encountered a financial predator?

Question: Do you have any friends or family whom you believe could be financial predators?

Question: If you are with a group of friends are you careful about not disclosing or discussing your **NEW** with them?

Question: Do you take care and make sure that you do not disclose your date of birth, social security number or other personal financial information on line or to people on the telephone that you do not know?

Question: What would you do if your credit card was stolen?

Question: What would you do if your identity was stolen?

A NEW Focus on

Bananas

A NEW FOCUS ON BANANAS

- BANANA TYPE # 1: ADDICTION

- BANANA TYPE # 2: JAIL

- BANANA TYPE # 3: CHEATING

- BANANA TYPE # 4: LIES, LIES, AND EVEN MORE LIES

- BANANA TYPE # 5: CHILD MOLESTER

- BANANA TYPE # 6: DOMESTIC ABUSE

> You can't straighten out a Banana! This FOCUS is designed to help you recognize the Bananas in your life and give you the courage to deal with them!

Let's get started!

You can't straighten out a Banana

Accept this and move on.
Don't waste YOUR life trying to straighten out a Banana.

There is no question in my mind that some people are simply that. Bananas! You can't straighten them out. Sadly, at any age you can find yourself married to a Banana. The saying is that Love is Blind and unfortunately, this is exactly how you end up with a Banana in your life.

HOT TIP: Whatever you do please do not marry a Banana! Do not even take a chance! Instead, simply live together if you are bent on being involved with the Banana!

BANANA TYPE # 1: ADDICTION

* Drug abuse and alcohol are not the only addictions that exist. There are both women and men who are addicted to sex, gambling, and squandering money. Counseling may help.

* Chances are that you will probably wake up one day realizing that you gave up everything for what?

    ✔ Move on!

* Stay friends if it makes sense for the children, but make sure that the children have counseling so that they see the warning signs and can call you to be picked up, if need be, while visiting your ex-Banana.

BANANA TYPE # 2: JAIL

* What are you going to do if your spouse goes to jail for 15–20 years?

    ✔ Move on!

* Stay friends if it makes sense for the children.

* Make sure that the children receive counseling. They have to deal with this, too.

NOTES

BANANA TYPE # 3: CHEATING

* Once a cheater, always a cheater, according to the textbooks! Maybe forgive once and then…

  ✔ Move on!

* Stay friends if it makes sense for the children!

BANANA TYPE # 4: LIES, LIES, AND EVEN MORE LIES

* Nothing like a Banana liar. When they are lying to you, they actually believe that they are telling you the truth.

* If it is affecting your **NEW**…

  ✔ Move on!

* You can stay friends! But, stay out of any financial dealings with them!

BANANA TYPE # 5: CHILD MOLESTER

* Do not bury your head in the sand. It is not fair to your children. Face up to it. Do not stay friends!

  ✔ Move on!

BANANA TYPE # 6: DOMESTIC ABUSE

* You are constantly made to feel that you are to blame. For what?

* Help your spouse get counseling and, if it does not work pretty quickly…

  ✔ Move on!

* Kick 'em out and do not stay friends!

NOTES

Question: Has this FOCUS helped to understand the concept of Banana people?

Question: Have you ever dated a Banana?

Question: Do you understand why it is better to get rid of the romantic Bananas in your life rather than have them drag you down and out financially?

Question: Do you have friends that are Bananas?

Question: Have you thought about whether you should get rid of Banana friends in your life?

NEW FINANCIAL WISDOM

CHOOSE YOUR PROFESSIONAL DIVORCE TEAM WISELY!
Just remember that when you either sign or get hit with those divorce papers, you probably will not be able to use the same professionals whom you and your spouse have been using for years.
OUCH!

A NEW Focus on

Identifying Capable Professionals

A **NEW** FOCUS ON IDENTIFYING CAPABLE PROFESSIONALS

- **ATTORNEYS**

- **CERTIFIED PUBLIC ACCOUNTANT (CPA)**

- **INSURANCE AGENTS**

- **VERIFYING CREDENTIALS**

- **INVESTMENT PROFESSIONALS WHO WILL ACTUALLY INVEST YOUR SAVINGS**

If you have an inkling that you may be heading down the path towards a divorce, it's good to know how to find the right professionals for your team. This FOCUS is designed to help you with this. Just remember that it's not necessarily the best pit bull professional who wins the day for you in a divorce – it more often than not is the best poker player.

Let's get started!

During your lifetime, you will undoubtedly have to deal with many professionals. Hiring an unethical or incompetent professional is a risk that you need to try to avoid!

- ✔ Clearly understand how you will pay for their services.
- ✔ Make sure that they are licensed in the state!
- ✔ Make sure they have at least 10 years of experience!
- ✔ Interview them. Use a checklist if necessary.
- ✔ Ask questions about their backgrounds.
- ✔ Ask people you respect for recommendations.
- ✔ Clearly understand the service you are buying.
- ✔ Clearly understand how you will be charged and pay for their services.

ATTORNEYS

- ❂ Attorneys graduate from law school after which they must pass an exam administered by the American Bar Association in order to become licensed to practice.

- ❂ Attorneys usually practice in special areas of interest, and they can sit exams to give them recognition as specialists in these areas.

- ❂ A divorce lawyer is a legal professional who specializes in issues pertaining to divorce, including divorce, dissolution, and annulment. Most divorce lawyers are family law practitioners.

- ❂ Should you hire a large law firm to handle your divorce or can you work with smaller firm or even a sole practitioner? The answer to this lies in the type of legal help that you need. Some small law firms are quite capable of doing the same work as a large law firm.

- ❂ A must-know is that you should NOT hire a lawyer specializing in Divorces to write your will or close on real estate UNLESS that lawyer also has expertise in these areas.

- ❂ Ask the attorney for an engagement letter that spells out what they will do for you and how much they will charge. You need to know their hourly billing rate, and you need to have them bill you regularly (monthly) so that you know how much they are digging into your NEW.

- ❂ DO NOT draft legal documents yourself. Sooner or later you will wish that you had not done this and had instead spent the money on a competent attorney.

NOTES

USE THESE WEBSITES TO VERIFY A PROFESSIONAL'S CREDENTIALS

PROFESSION	RESOURCE	NOTES
Attorney	http://www.floridabar.org/	Verify through your state's bar association
CPA	http://www.myfloridalicense.com/dbpr/	Verify through your state board of accountancy
IRS Agent	http://www.irs.gov/localcontacts/index.html	Request the name and ID number of the agent in question. Verify with your local IRS branch.
Real Estate Agent	http://www.myfloridalicense.com/dbpr/	Verify through your state
Insurance Agent	http://www.flofr.com/consumer/verify.aspx	
PFS	http://apps.alcpa.org/credentialsrefweb/pfscredentialsearchpage.aspx	
CFP	http://www.cfp..net/find/enhancedsearch.aspx	
CFA	http://www.cfainstitute.org/about/membership/pages/member_directory.aspx	
Financial Advisors	www.finra.org	
Broker Dealers	www.sec.gov/investor/brokers.htm	

NOTES

CERTIFIED PUBLIC ACCOUNTANT (CPA)

● The American Institute of CPAs is the organization that sets standards for the CPA profession. These standards are then adopted by the individual state boards of accountancy.

● Make sure that you understand their billing structure and their hourly rate. Insist that you receive an engagement letter and a monthly invoice for the work that they are doing for you.

 INSURANCE AGENTS

● Make sure that they specialize in your needed area of insurance, whether it be Life, Disability, Long Term Care, Property, or Casualty Insurance.

● Before you buy annuities from a life insurance agent, make sure to discuss the product with your financial advisor. Insurance products, which include annuities, are highly commissioned products. Often the wrong product is identified and sold for the commissions alone and so be very careful.

NOTES

INVESTMENT PROFESSIONALS WHO WILL ACTUALLY INVEST YOUR SAVINGS

Professionals who actually invest your savings have to be licensed by the state and the Securities Exchange Commission (SEC). The SEC develops and administers a series of exams that investment professional have to pass. Each exam has a specific purpose and licenses the professional to deal with specific investment products and services. When working with a financial advisor think about:

- How much experience does the financial advisor have?

- Discuss your goals and objectives with the financial advisor. Ask the financial advisor to help you plan for both your current and future financial goals.

- Discuss how he or she is to be paid.

  - Fee only

      - ✔ Financial Planning: Hourly Fee
      - ✔ Portfolio Management: Percentage of "assets under management"

  - Commission basis only: Some investment professionals work on a commission basis only, and there is a transaction charge for each trade or product purchased.

  - Combination: From time to time, a fee-based professional may be forced to sell a product that is only offered on a commission basis. Some variable annuity products are a typical example.

Once the interview is over, say thank you. Then, consider doing the same thing with at least two other financial advisors. Take the time to find an advisor who is the right fit. Do your research and make sure the person you choose has the experience, expertise, and ethics that suits you.

NOTES

A NEW Focus on

YOUR Responsibilities

A NEW Focus on Your Responsibilities

One of the problems with marriage is that, when you put that ring on your finger and said "I DO," absent a prenuptial agreement, you have in effect signed away your 100% right to control the construction of a secure financial future for yourself.

Marriage is meant to be built on trust. But what happens when you find yourself with a "banana" spendthrift spouse and you end up responsible for 50% of their wasteful spending and the resulting debt?

HOT TIP: Keep your wits about you at all times and don't let this take place to begin with! It takes years and sometimes the rest of your life to recover from a bad financial decision!

> ✔ Acknowledging the risks that come with marriage and developing a solid plan for your financial future is the first step toward preparedness.

After reading Bridal Boot Camp you should be now better equipped to achieve YOUR goals whether you are newly engaged, married, or single. Before and after the "I DO's," a financially independent person will stand up for themselves and protect their **NEW** at all times and manifest the retirement that they want for themselves.

Below you will find a list of important responsibilities that you must accept in order to become financially independent.

> ✔ Try to burn these responsibilities in your brain and take each one seriously.

RESPONSIBILITIES THAT YOU WILL ACCEPT AS YOURS

- **YOU** will accept the responsibility for your own financial future.
- **YOU** will make it your duty to know **YOUR** property rights in the state where you reside.
- **YOU** will keep focused on **YOUR NEW**.
- **YOU** understand that **YOU** are responsible for saving and investing wisely.
- **YOU** will monitor **YOUR** investments to make sure that **YOUR** plan is on track.
- **YOU** will fight to protect your **NEW** in the event of a divorce.
- **YOU** will have constructive financial conversations with your spouse.
- **YOU** will take time to plan for **YOUR** current and future financial goals.
- **YOU** will create a budget and do your best to adhere to it.
- **YOU** will look for value in everything that you buy and avoid wasteful spending.
- **YOU** will avoid incurring senseless and potentially harmful debt.
- **YOU** will understand and respect your spouse's financial personalities.
- **YOU** will make sure that at all times **YOU** are properly protecting **YOUR** financial future and taking responsibility for reaching **YOUR** financial goals.
- **YOU** will be responsible for protecting **YOURSELF** and your family from emergencies with a cash reserve fund and adequate insurance.
- **YOU** will not stay trapped in a dysfunctional relationship.
- **YOU** will not be victim to financial predators and unethical professionals.
- **YOU** will hire competent portfolio managers to invest your **NEW**.

Learning from

THESE ARE SOME OF THE LOWEST CARDS IN A DECK AND THIS HAND IS GOING NOWHERE.

YOU DON'T HAVE TO ACCEPT THE HAND YOU WERE DEALT. KNOW WHEN TO FOLD AND GET OUT AND CUT YOUR LOSSES.

REAL LIFE
Tricks and Tragedies

LEARNING FROM REAL LIFE TRICKS AND TRAGEDIES

🐚 **CASE #1: MAJOR PURCHASE WITHOUT THOUGHT ABOUT HOW TO PAY FOR IT**

🐚 **CASE # 2: SIGNATURE ON THE HOME MORTGAGE AND NOT ON THE TITLE**

🐚 **CASE # 3: PRENUPTIAL AGREEMENT GAMES**

🐚 **CASE # 4: NOT PROTECTING YOURSELF WITH LIFE INSURANCE**

🐚 **CASE # 5: FINANCIAL PREDATOR**

🐚 **CASE # 6: CREDIT CARD DEBT**

🐚 **CASE # 7: WIFE UNPREPARED TO HANDLE FINANCIAL FUTURE AFTER DIVORCE**

🐚 **CASE # 8: WIFE CLEANS OUT THE SAFETY DEPOSIT BOX**

🐚 **CASE # 9: LIVING TOGETHER FOR 25 YEARS BEFORE GETTING MARRIED**

🐚 **CASE # 10: ALIMONY NOT PAID BY HUSBAND**

There is nothing better than real life experiences to reinforce the risks and realities embedded in marriage! Love may be blind but that does not mean that you have to be financially blindsided! This FOCUS is designed to help you stay alert and teach you that it is all right for you to put your foot down when you have to. Nothing says that you have to be another financial failure statistic! Keep building your **NEW** and don't let anyone stand in your way! Keep your eye on that Red Ball!

Let's get started!

CASE # 1: MAJOR PURCHASE WITHOUT THOUGHT ABOUT HOW TO PAY FOR IT

Your husband decides that the family should buy a $75,000 boat because "the family" will have so much fun using it. He decides that the best way to finance the boat is by using a Home Equity Line of Credit (HELOC) on the family residence that happens to be in his name only. He asks you to sign a mortgage note to pay for the boat. The HELOC (Home Equity Line of Credit) is an "Interest Only" loan with no schedule for repayment of the principal.

The family soon discovers that the cost of running the boat is expensive because of repairs and gas prices and that, to enjoy this "toy", all other forms of family entertainment have to cease.

Soon, the novelty of owning the boat wears off, and the family becomes bored with it. Problems soon arise because the financial burden of owning the "toy" has created added financial pressure to the family budget. You are trapped because, although the boat has been paid for in full, you still have to make monthly payments on the HELOC.

HOW IT ENDED

In the case of the boat, the couple got a divorce. At the time of the divorce, the boat was worth $7,500 and the HELOC still had a balance of $ 71,500.

The husband took the boat in settlement and, of course, the wife had 50% of the debt subtracted from her side of the family NEW.

WHAT ARE THE DYNAMICS GOING ON?
1 Easy access to money
2 Not thinking through how the boat loan would be paid off

🐚 **QUESTION # 1**: What is the impact of buying a boat on your NEW, over time?

🐚 **QUESTION # 2**: What is the impact of borrowing without a plan to repay the loan?

🐚 **QUESTION # 3**: Who is responsible for repaying the HELOC?

🐚 **QUESTION # 4**: What is the net impact on your NEW if the boat is sold for $7,500?

🐚 **QUESTION # 5**: What conversation should you have before buying a boat or other major depreciable asset?

CASE # 2: SIGNATURE ON THE HOME MORTGAGE AND NOT ON THE TITLE

You have been divorced once and are now newly married to your second husband. Your new husband was also divorced before you married him. He has three children. You have one child.

You were forced to sell your house due to your divorce and have been living in an appartment.

Your new husband owns a nice home worth about $ 775,000. You move into the house after you are married. Your husband owes $500,000 on the home.

You did not sign a pre-marital agreement before you married your husband.

Your husband has a decent job with nice retirement benefits, and so do you. You are both still working.

However, you would not be able to afford to maintain the current residence on your own.

Interest rates start to drop, and your husband comes to you and says that he would like to refinance the house to take advantage of the lower interest rates.

The bank is happy to give your husband a loan BUT insists that you sign on to the mortgage note because the house has now become homestead property.

The end result is that your signature ends up on the $500,000 mortgage but not on the title of the house.

QUESTION # 1: Do you think that this lady was smart to end up in this situation? What would you have done differently?

QUESTION # 2: If you are a Florida resident and your husband dies, what rights do you have in the house? Remember, title to the house is in HIS name alone.

QUESTION # 3: If your husband dies, how are you going to get yourself out of this mess?

CASE # 3: PRENUPTIAL AGREEMENT GAMES

a month before you get married your future husband asks you to sign a prenuptial agreement. You are in shock.

Your attorney advises you not to sign the agreement. You are too embarrassed to cancel your marriage plans because wedding invitations have already been sent out.

Against the wishes of your attorney, you sign away all current and future financial interests in all of his assets including your marital rights in the home that you are sharing which is in his name solely. You are 37 when you get married.

You think that the homestead is fully paid for, but in anticipation of the upcoming marriage and request for a prenuptial agreement, a mortgage for 100% of the value of the house is placed on the homestead. The money is borrowed from a partnership in which your future spouse has an interest.

You really do not have a flourishing career although you dabble in decorating and make a little money doing this. You could probably support yourself if you had to, but you would have to work very hard and this would not be particularly good for your marriage.

Your husband frequently travels and does not want you to work. He wants you to travel with him.

You have lunch with a girlfriend who advises you that you should never have signed the agreement and she advises you to start nagging your husband to at least let you start to build equity in the homestead.

Your new husband is a sharp business man and eventually agrees for you to be on the title of the house. When this takes place you also have to sign on to the mortgage note.

The house is now worth $280,000 and there is a mortgage of $280,000 on it. At this point in time, the house has no equty in it.

Two years later you are not getting along with your new husband and in fact, you now hate his guts and you decide to divorce him. You think that you will share equally in the value of the house.

You are shocked to discover that you own 50% of NOTHING since there is no equity in the house.

You decide to walk away in disgust rather than waste more time and effort fighting him. In fact you call an old boy friend and move in with him and live very happily after that.

Your former spouse goes through a couple of more wives!

QUESTION # 1: What financial conversation should you have had with your future husband BEFORE you sent out wedding invitations?

QUESTION # 2: Are you comfortable with working out a prenuptial agreement before you get married and if not why not?

QUESTION # 3: Why do you think that anyone would want to compromise their financial future by signing away all of their marital rights in a marriage especially when they are going to be a homemaker for the convenience of their spouse?

QUESTION # 4: How on earth was this wife ever going to build a financial future for herself if she was asked not to work?

CASE # 4: NOT PROTECTING YOURSELF WITH LIFE INSURANCE

Your husband is getting ready to retire. You are both in your early fifties. You have mainly been a housewife since your marriage and raised the children. Your husband has two retirement plan options.

Plan # 1: He can receive a pension which will pay a lifetime income for both of you.

Plan # 2: He can receive get a much larger pension, but this will only pay a guaranteed lifetime income until your husband dies.

The union suggests that if an employee is not going to exercise Plan 2, that the employee first buys an income replacement life insurance policy on their life for the surviving spouse.

Your husband's friends tell him that they have all opted for Plan # 2 and will worry about dying later.

Your husband retires before taking out an income-replacement life insurance policy to protect you in the event that he is the first to die. Later, when your husband does attempt to take out a policy, he gets some bad news. He is not insurable.

One of the reasons that he failed to take out the income-replacement insurance policy before he made the decision to use Plan # 2 is because he decided to buy a boat that he had always dreamed of owning when he retired.

Fifteen years later, your husband dies of a heart attack and you are left with no insurance, a house and a small mortgage, no pension and, of course, the boat.

The boat is worthless; you donate the boat so that you don't have to pay for insurance any longer.

QUESTION # 1: Was this wife protecting her financial future by not putting her foot down?

QUESTION # 2: What should the wife have insisted her husband do before making his final decision?

QUESTION # 3: Since it is your husband's pension and you have been basically a housewife during the entire marriage, would you feel uncomfortable having a constructive financial conversation with your husband about which option to choose?

QUESTION # 4: Would it have been smart for the wife to insist that her husband get a medical evaluation before he signed up for Plan # 2?

QUESTION # 5: What type of life insurance policy would have been suitable in this situation?

CASE # 5: FINANCIAL PREDATOR

You are single and a busy lady. You are charmed by a man who woos you and tells you that he thinks that you should be in business for yourself.

You buy a small business and start working 24/7 to make it work. You are seeing positive results because you are talented.

In the meantime, your boyfriend is helping you by running the office and keeping the books for you so that you can work harder in the business.

Your parents are elderly and need your help writing checks and doing other banking chores for them and you and your sisters help them with this.

Soon, your boyfriend comes to you and suggests that your parents sign a power of attorney so that he can help them when you are too busy to do this.

Everyone in the family thinks this is a great idea.

Wrong. One year later you find out the following:

1. Your parent's 401(k), which was the source of their retirement income, is gone, picked clean by your boyfriend.
2. You find that your parents' mortgage-free house now has a substantial mortgage on it.
3. You only own 49% of your business. Your boyfriend, who put no cash into it, owns 51%.
4. You find out that lover boy has done this before.

You find that the Sheriff's Office and the State Attorney's office are of very little help.

QUESTION # 1: Stupid! Stupid! Stupid! Where were the checks and balances?

QUESTION # 2: Do you think that, if this lady had known what she needed to do to secure a solid financial future, she might have been more careful about allowing someone to consume her life so easily?

QUESTION # 3: How much attention do you need to personally pay to your business and other personal financial matters?

QUESTION # 4: Who do you think that you can trust with your financial future?

CASE # 6: CREDIT CARD DEBT

You are 30 and you get married to a gentleman with a promising career. You are both working and plan to eventually have a family.

When you get married, you open a joint bank account. Each of you contributes $500. This is the extent of your wealth, you think!

Your conversations before you got married were about saving for a house and eventually starting a family. After six months of marriage, you discover that your husband brought a substantial amount of credit card debt into the marriage that was not disclosed to you. It amounts to about $20,000. You believe him when he says he did not tell you because he loved you so much and was scared that you would not marry him.

You give up having spending money of your own, take your entire paycheck each pay period, and pay down the debt until it is fully paid off. All is well, and you and your husband agree that this is now a fresh start for both of you.

You get a nasty surprise one day when your husband accidentally leaves a credit card statement in his jacket pocket. You are stunned when you realize he has changed the address on the account, so that all of his new credit card's monthly statements have been going to his office.

You are shattered. Unfortunately, you still love your husband--but not quite as much as when you first got married!

QUESTION # 1: Does your husband have a spending addiction problem? Is your husband a banana?

QUESTION # 2: What are you going to do to turn this situation around and build a secure financial future for yourself?

QUESTION # 3: What financial conversation are you going to have with your husband about YOUR financial future?

QUESTION # 4: How could you have found out about your husband's outstanding credit card debt before you got married?

QUESTION # 5: Do you think that a couple should disclose to each other, before marriage, their credit report, tax returns and information about all of their assets, liabilities, income and expenses?

NOTE: This is a real situation except it was the wife who had the credit card debt problem. The marriage eventually ended in divorce. After racking up a third round of credit card debt, the husband decided that he would end up with nothing if he continued to stay married to this wife.

CASE # 7: WIFE UNPREPARED TO HANDLE FINANCIAL FUTURE AFTER DIVORCE

A couple gets married and, after 25 years of marriage, decide to get divorced because they have grown apart.

The wife has been a housewife during the entire marriage and raised the family.

The wife is 55 when the divorce occurs, and she receives a $1,500,000 settlement when the divorce is final. The settlement consists of $500,000 in cash and her $1,000,000 interest in her husband's employer retirement plan.

The wife's attorney arranges for a QDRO, and the wife's retirement plan settlement is rolled into an Individual Retirement Account.

The wife lets an old boyfriend start to direct her spending, and he lines his pockets with her wealth.

Five years later, the wife has very little left. She has literally blown through her entire divorce settlement. On top of everything else, she owes some serious money to the IRS. She goes to work for a fast food chain to help make ends meet.

QUESTION # 1: What is going on here?

QUESTION # 2: What would you have done differently?

QUESTION # 3: At age 55, could the wife have retired on $1,500,000 and lived comfortably?

CASE # 8: WIFE CLEANS OUT SAFETY DEPOSIT BOX

A couple gets married and after many years the husband's mother dies. The husband is an only child.

The husband inherits about $175,000 worth of jewelry and other valuable small gold objects from his mother's estate and places them in a safety deposit box at the bank. The box is titled in his sole name.

The husband has been married for just over 10 years and the bank suggests that he consider making the safety deposit box a joint account with his wife so that in case he dies she will have access to the box. He does this.

Five years later, the husband decides to surprise his wife with a special gift for Christmas. He makes arrangements with his jeweler to exchange some of the gold jewelry in the safety deposit box for a beautiful new piece of jewelry for his wife.

The husband goes to the bank with a smile on his face but when he opens up the safety deposit box he finds it EMPTY! Bank records show that his wife was the last one to access the safety deposit box.

THE ENDING: This marriage ended very soon after in a nasty divorce.

QUESTION # 1: What is going on here?

QUESTION # 2: Instead of owning the safety deposit box jointly with his wife, should the husband have considered opening the safety deposit box account using a Transfer on Death (TOD) title? This would have denied the wife access to the box during the husband's lifetime but given her access to the box after his death.

QUESTION # 3: What did the wife do with the gold jewelry? What did she spend all of this money on? Surely the husband had to notice that there was more money being spent than he and his wife were earning? Where was his head at?

QUESTION #4: Could a budget have pin pointed that something was out of whack with the family finances?

CASE # 9 LIVING TOGETHER FOR 25 YEARS BEFORE GETTING MARRIED

Husband is a devout Catholic and does not want to get remarried as long as his first wife is still alive.

Husband's first wife eventually dies and the husband proposes to and marries his devoted companion of 25 years.

Husband is 67 and his new wife is 50.

Husband arranges to immediately retitle most of his assets to joint tenants with the right of survivorship (JTWROS). His new wife now owns 50% of most of his assets.

Two years later the marriage ends in a nasty divorce and the husband wakes up to the harsh reality that his beloved companion who is now his new ex-wife has "cleaned his financial clock"!

There was no prenuptial agreement.

QUESTION # 1: What is going on here?

QUESTION # 2: Should the husband have considered a prenuptial agreement before getting married?

CASE # 10 ALIMONY NOT PAID BY HUSBAND

Husband and wife are negotiating a divorce.

Husbands insists that he needs all of the family cash as working capital to salvage his failing business enterprise. In return, husband agrees to pay his soon to be ex-wife alimony for a period of 5 years. The amount of alimony to be paid to the wife amounts to 50% of the family cash.

Wife accepts this arrangement in spite of her divorce attorney's advice not to do this.

Wife also receives some other very illiquid assets in the divorce.

When the divorce is finally over, the wife finds herself without a cash reserve fund.

Husband pays the wife alimony payments for 6 months and then stops making payments.

The divorce decree has no provisions for penalties to be levied against the husband for non-payment of alimony.

The wife finds herself trapped. The legal costs of fighting over the alimony payments are expensive and she has no cash with which to fight this battle.

QUESTION # 1: Why do you think that the wife did not listen to her attorney's advice?

QUESTION # 2: Should the wife have insisted on attaching assets belonging to her husband to guarantee the payment of alimony?

QUESTION # 3: If there were no other assets available for the wife to attach and in order to guarantee the husband's payment of alimony, should the wife have insisted on taking at least 50% of the cash in the marital estate as part of the divorce settlement?

Goodbye
is your NEW
Beginning

All of our Boot camps relate back to helping you understand how important it is to financially protect yourself by keeping an eye and focus on protecting your NEW and the future growth of your NEW at all times.

In closing I want to leave you with an important thought. Over the years you may have heard people say that they want to become "financially independent".

Financial independence is a state of mind, and although you may not have realized it, one of the main objectives of Bridal Financial Boot Camp has been to educate you on HOW you can start moving forward with a NEW FOCUS and MINDSET on earning, saving, investing and accumulating wealth. You too can become financially independent!

- Financial independence **is not financial security** – because you can lose your financial security in a split second.

- Financially independent people can lose EVERYTHING they own and still be able to pick themselves up and rebuild their NEW by simply deploying the essential building block principals taught in this course.

- Financial independence is a NEW MINDSET. Once you have grasped it and have the tools in your possession, you cannot lose it. No one can ever take it away from you.

- Understanding the importance of focusing on your NEW constantly and using strategies to grow and protect it will help you become financially independent for the rest of your life.

HOT TIP: Use the checklists provided on the next pages to ensure you are on the path toward financial independence whether you are starting out in a new marriage or on your own.

HOT TIP: If you have enjoyed Bridal Financial Boot Camp and would like to gain an even deeper understanding on how to grow your NEW, consider reading *The Essentials for Accumulating and Preserving Wealth*. This book is also enjoyable and fun to read.

We never say Goodbye.

Even our Goodbye FOCUS contains great wisdom for you!

CHECKLIST: TO DO BEFORE YOU SAY "I DO"

☐ **Review the assets of your future spouse**

- ☐ Do they have a checking account?
- ☐ Do they have a savings account?
- ☐ Do they have an emergency fund?
- ☐ Do they have an investment brokerage account?
- ☐ Do they have any retirement accounts?
- ☐ Do they own any annuities?
- ☐ Do they own a home?
- ☐ Do they own investments in real estate?

☐ **Review the debts and liabilities of your future spouse**

- ☐ Do they have outstanding student loan debt?
- ☐ Do they have outstanding credit card debt?
- ☐ Do they have an outstanding car loan?
- ☐ Do they have an outstanding boat loan?
- ☐ Do they have an outstanding mortgage?
- ☐ Do they have any personal debts?

☐ **Discuss with your future spouse their current income and how much of their income they are currently allocating to saving**

☐ **Discuss whether you will be keeping your finances separate or combining them**

☐ **Discuss your wills and have a conversation over who will inherit the money should one of you die prematurely**

☐ **Discuss shared future financial goals, and how you will jointly save to reach them**

☐ **Ask about your fiance's credit history. Will your fiance's credit score be a problem in the future?**

☐ **Discuss ways you may increase income in the future to increase savings**

Would additional education help you to earn a higher income?

Would moving to a different location provide better employment options?

Does initially prioritizing one spouses career over the other's make sense?

☐ **Come up with an itemized budget that you both agree on**

CHECKLIST: CONVERSATIONS ONCE YOU ARE MARRIED

- ☐ **Are you scheduling financial meetings with your spouse at least once or twice a year, and taking notes at these meetings?**

- ☐ **Are you on track to reach the future financial goals you both laid out?**

- ☐ **Are you monitoring together how your NEW is growing over time?**

- ☐ **Are you sticking with your agreed upon budget? If you are deviating from the budget:**

  - ☐ Determine whether one or both spouses is overspending
  - ☐ Discuss the reasons for overspending and agree on a solution
  - ☐ Adjust the budget, if necessary, for changes in circumstances
  - ☐ Consider automatically deducting savings from your paychecks so that you are keeping this money out of easy reach

- ☐ **Does one spouse control the family purse strings and monitor the NEW? If one spouse is in charge, make sure the other spouse:**

  - ☐ Knows about the existence of each major family asset
  - ☐ Knows how to access all family assets in the event of an emergency
  - ☐ Understands the tax consequences of tapping into these assets

- ☐ **Are you adequately insured (life and disability) so that if the unthinkable were to occur, the surviving spouse would not be financially burdened?**

- ☐ **Do the beneficiaries on your insurance and retirement assets reflect both of your current wishes?**

- ☐ **Are there employment opportunities available that may help to increase household income?**

- ☐ **Are both spouses comfortable with the family's financial direction?**

- ☐ **Do both spouses understand the basic tenants of wealth accumulation and preservation?**

CHECKLIST: CONVERSATIONS WITH A BABY ON THE WAY

- ☐ **Re-assess the amount of life and disability insurance that each spouse is carrying - an insurance agent can help**
- ☐ **Have an attorney make relevant changes to your wills and beneficiary designations**
- ☐ **Consider who you will want appointed guardian for your child should death or incapacity unexpectedly happen to both spouses**
- ☐ **Consider appointing a separate financial guardian for your child should one spouse die and the other spouse is not financially responsible**
- ☐ **Re-visit your budget and make sure to include baby-related changes**
  - ☐ Will you need to send the child to day care or hire a nanny?
  - ☐ Will one of the spouses be giving up their career to raise the child?
  - ☐ Have you considered additional incidental costs - diapers, food, etc.
  - ☐ Consider beginning some type of college savings plan

- ☐ **Consider your support group in raising the child**
  - ☐ Do you have family in the area who can help with baby sitting?
  - ☐ Do you have supportive neighbors who might be able to help?

- ☐ **Review the maternity and paternity policies that your employers have, and decide how long a leave-of-absence you will take**
- ☐ **Review your health insurance policy to see what is and what is not covered under your policy**
- ☐ **If you need financial assistance due to medical costs from the pregnancy, look to local clinics and government programs for assistance**

Checklist

Additional Opportunities to Learn About Other **NEW** Wealth Focus Topics

A **NEW** Focus on: Risk Management

A **NEW** Focus on: Financial Predators

A **NEW** Focus on: Goals and Retirement Risks

A **NEW** Focus on: Income Tax Planning

A **NEW** Focus on: Investment Strategies

A **NEW** Focus on: Tax Deferred Savings and Annuities

A **NEW** Focus on: Buying is Spending, *Learn how to control it!*

A **NEW** Focus on: Choosing the Right Professionals

A **NEW** Focus on: Planning for the Future

    Part 1: Legacy Planning and Transfers

    Part 2: Estate and Gift Taxes

A NEW Focus on Risk Management

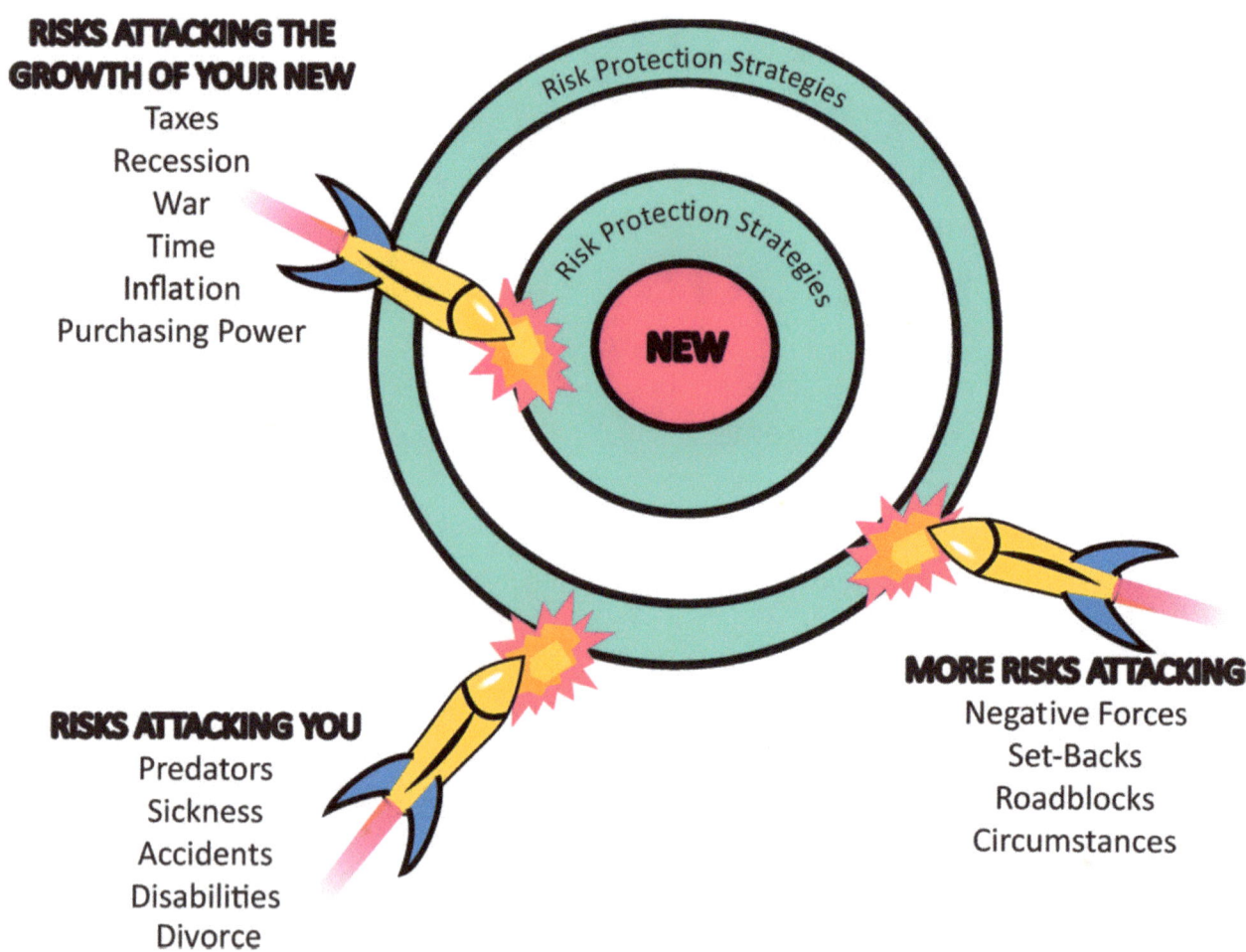

RISKS ATTACKING THE GROWTH OF YOUR NEW
Taxes
Recession
War
Time
Inflation
Purchasing Power

RISKS ATTACKING YOU
Predators
Sickness
Accidents
Disabilities
Divorce

MORE RISKS ATTACKING
Negative Forces
Set-Backs
Roadblocks
Circumstances

Risk Protection Strategies

Risk Protection Strategies

NEW

Course: A New Focus on Risk Management

Learn: The Essentials for Accumulating and Preserving Wealth only began to cover the risks you will face while growing and protecting your NEW. This book and online course will provide you with even more principles and strategies that you can use to combat these risks.

Who should attend?: Risk is everywhere and YOU need to prepared.

Register: www.Essentialwealthconcepts.com

A NEW Focus on Financial Predators

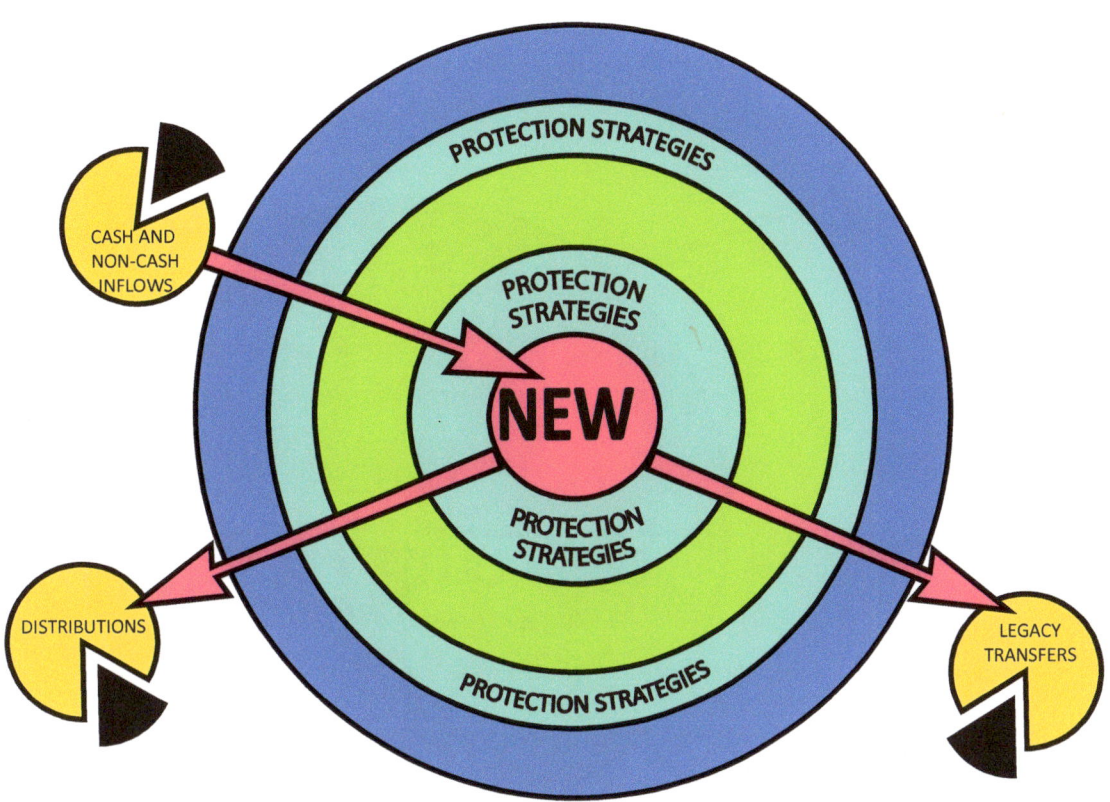

There are only 3 ways Predators can attack your NEW:

1 CASH AND NON-CASH INFLOWS
2 DISTRIBUTIONS
3 LEGACY TRANSFERS

Course: A New Focus on Financial Predators

Learn: Find out how to identify financial predators and implement tools and strategies to keep your NEW safe from them. Hear first hand accounts from victims and investigators on topics ranging from identity theft to manipulative family members.

Who should attend?: Senior financial abuse is the crime of the century. However, this book and online course will help people of all ages to identify behavior patterns of financial predators.

Register: www.Essentialwealthconcepts.com

A NEW Focus on Goals and Retirement Risks

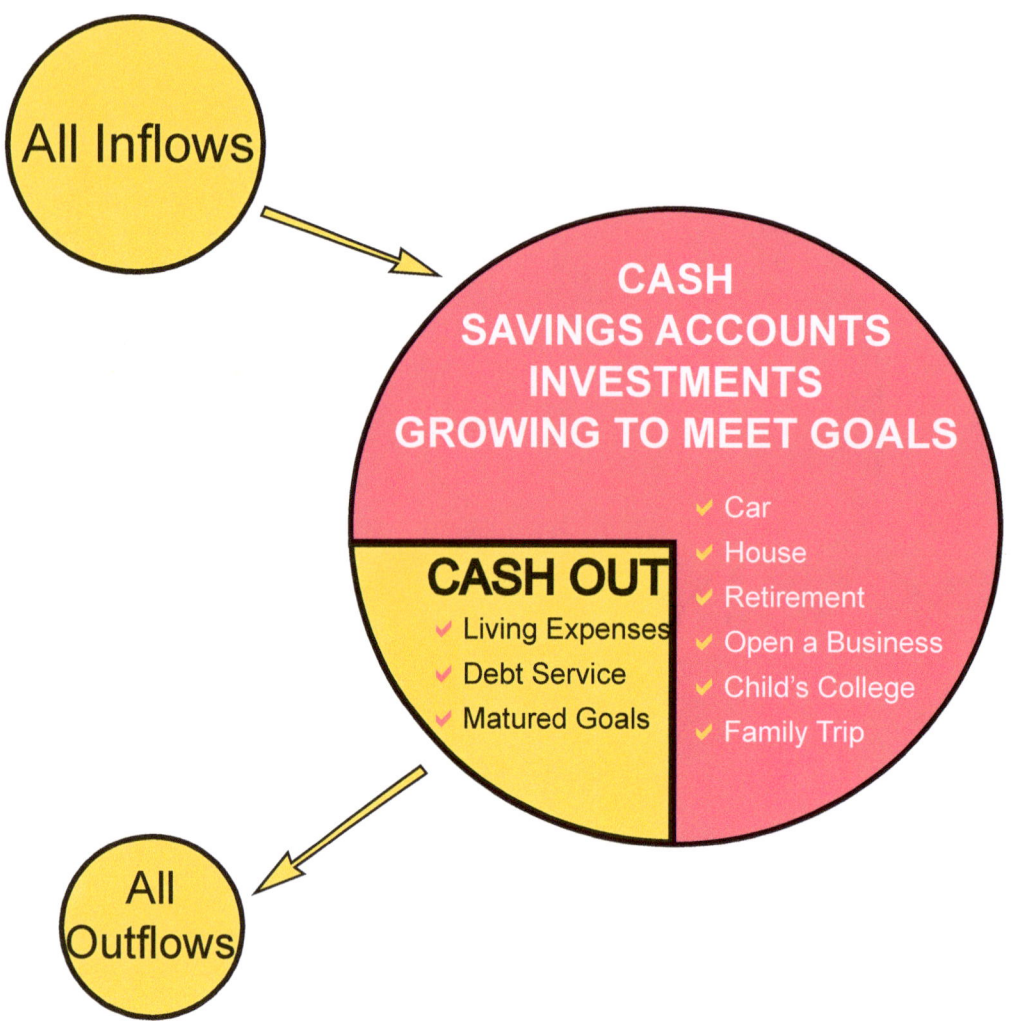

All Inflows

**CASH
SAVINGS ACCOUNTS
INVESTMENTS
GROWING TO MEET GOALS**

✓ Car
✓ House
✓ Retirement
✓ Open a Business
✓ Child's College
✓ Family Trip

CASH OUT
✓ Living Expenses
✓ Debt Service
✓ Matured Goals

All
Outflows

Course: A New Focus on Goals and Retirement Risks

Learn: Retirement is an AMOUNT not an AGE and should be considered as just another goal. Not only will this book and online course teach you the ins and outs of retirement and provide you with valuable tips but it includes retirement risks that will open your eyes to the unthinkable things that can go wrong during your retirement and totally derail you!

Who should attend: Everyone who wants to prepare for and live comfortably during retirement.

Register: www.Essentialwealthconcepts.com

Course: A New Focus on Tax Planning

Learn: When you pay income taxes it takes a permanent bite out of your **NEW**. $Poof $Gone. $Adios forever!

You need to understand federal and state income taxes so that you can plan to minimize the damage that it can do to your **NEW**. Find out how to protect your **NEW** with smart tax planning strategies. This book and online course will walk you through how to do this.

Who should attend?: Everyone! "The two things in life that you cannot escape are death and taxes."

Register: www.Essentialwealthconcepts.com

A NEW Focus on Investment Strategies

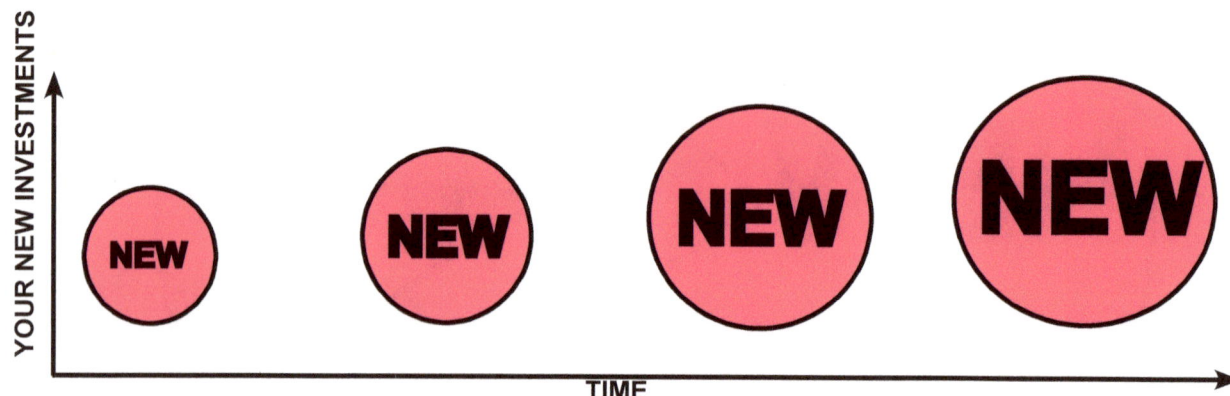

THE KEY TO WEALTH ACCUMULATION IS GROWING YOUR NEW.

Course: A New Focus on Investment Strategies

Learn: This investment planning book and online course will help you to understand the stock and bond markets and how they behave. It will also teach you about the risks and rewards associated with the market and many other aspects of investing. It is all about growing your NEW.

Who should attend?: Everyone will benefit from this book and online course. When investors lack a basic understanding of the market, this can come back to haunt them when tough decisions have to be made. After you have read this book you won't be saying to your investment advisor – "do what you think is best". You will be able to ask intelligent questions about your portfolio.

Register: www.Essentialwealthconcepts.com

A NEW Focus on Tax Deferred Savings and Annuities

INVESTMENT GROWTH STUNTED BY INCOME TAXES

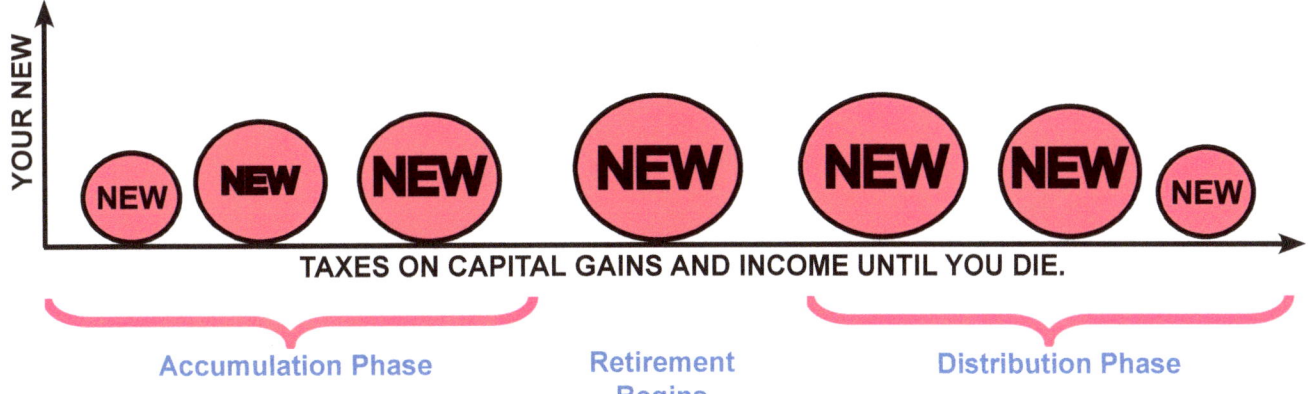

TAX FREE GROWTH OF INVESTMENTS

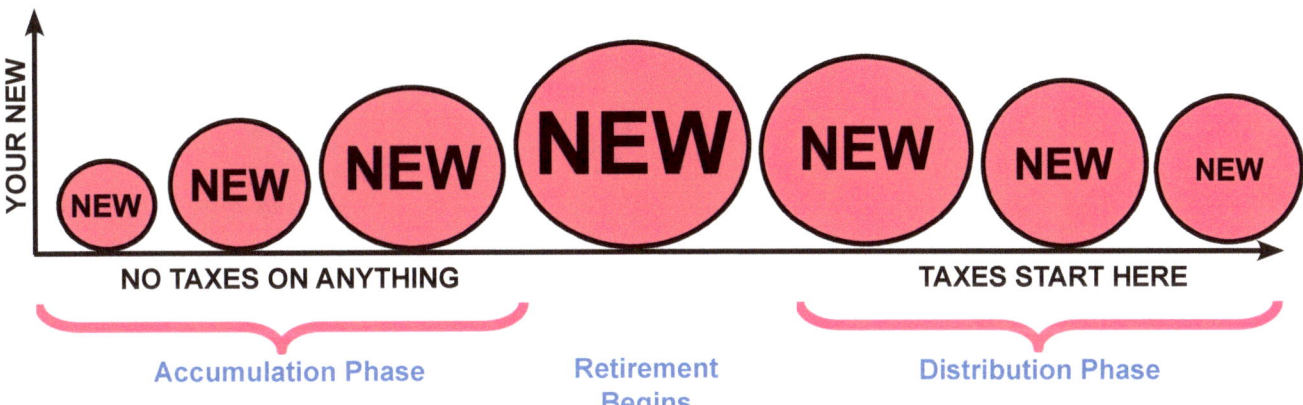

Course: A New Focus on Tax Deferred Savings and Annuities

Learn: How to utilize different tax deferred instruments such as retirement accounts and annuities. Learn how annuities provide other retirement income guaranteed by the underlying insurance company and at the same time provide asset protection.

Who should attend?: Anyone who wants to maximize the growth of their NEW for future retirement distributions.

Register: www.Essentialwealthconcepts.com

A NEW Focus on Buying is Spending

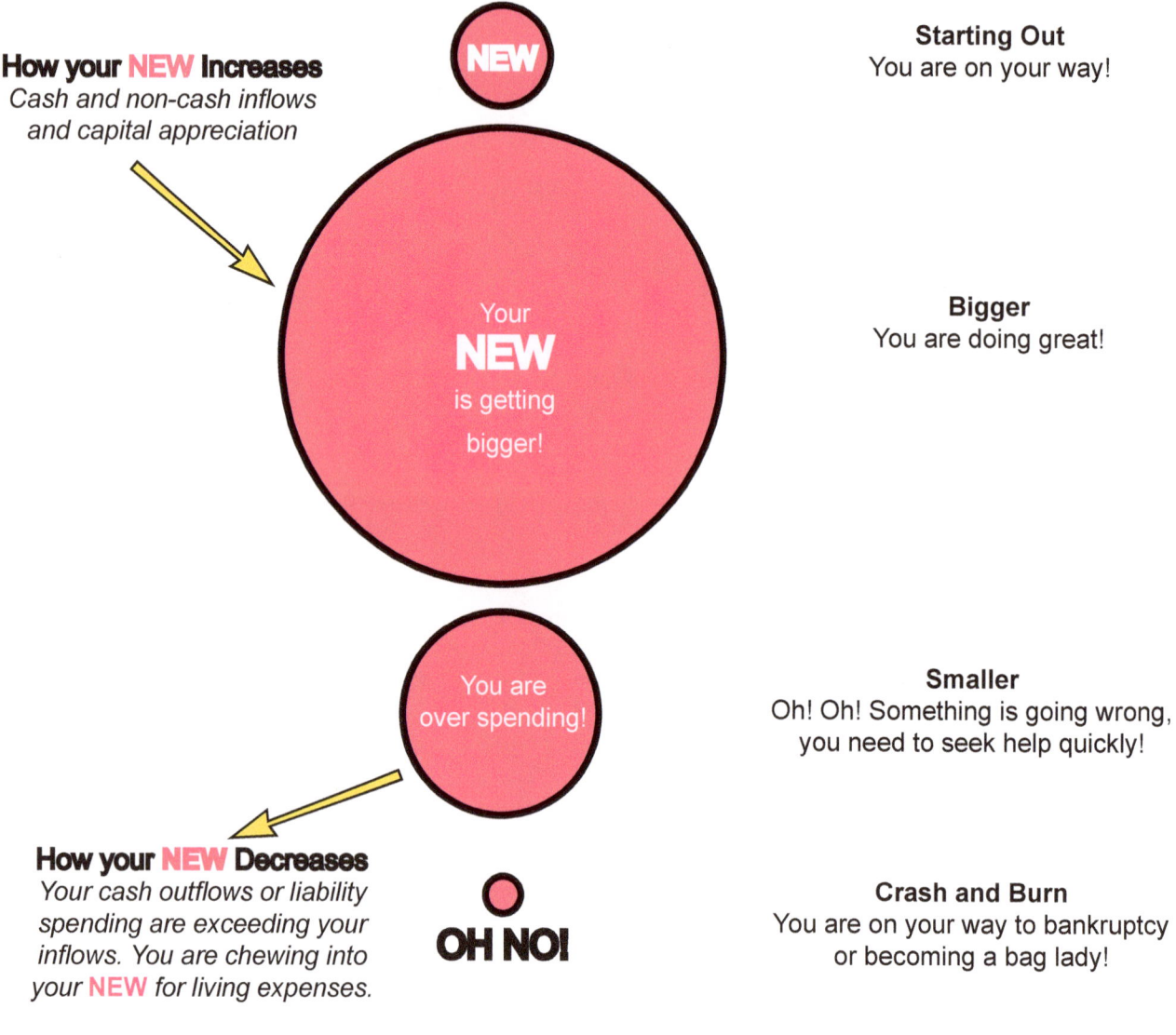

How your NEW Increases
Cash and non-cash inflows and capital appreciation

NEW

Your **NEW** is getting bigger!

You are over spending!

How your NEW Decreases
Your cash outflows or liability spending are exceeding your inflows. You are chewing into your NEW for living expenses.

OH NO!

Starting Out
You are on your way!

Bigger
You are doing great!

Smaller
Oh! Oh! Something is going wrong, you need to seek help quickly!

Crash and Burn
You are on your way to bankruptcy or becoming a bag lady!

Course: A New Focus on Buying is Spending

Learn: Spending money on unnecessary purchases is a common drain on people's **NEW**. Learn how to control your discretionary spending and make smart buying decisions on necessary living expenses. We will discuss how to grab the best deals on cars and boats, a home, real estate investments, and much more. If over spending is a problem, this book and online course will provide you with an in depth budget recap to control your spending.

Who should attend: Anyone who wants to learn how to buy smart and spend their **NEW** wisely.

Register: www.Essentialwealthconcepts.com

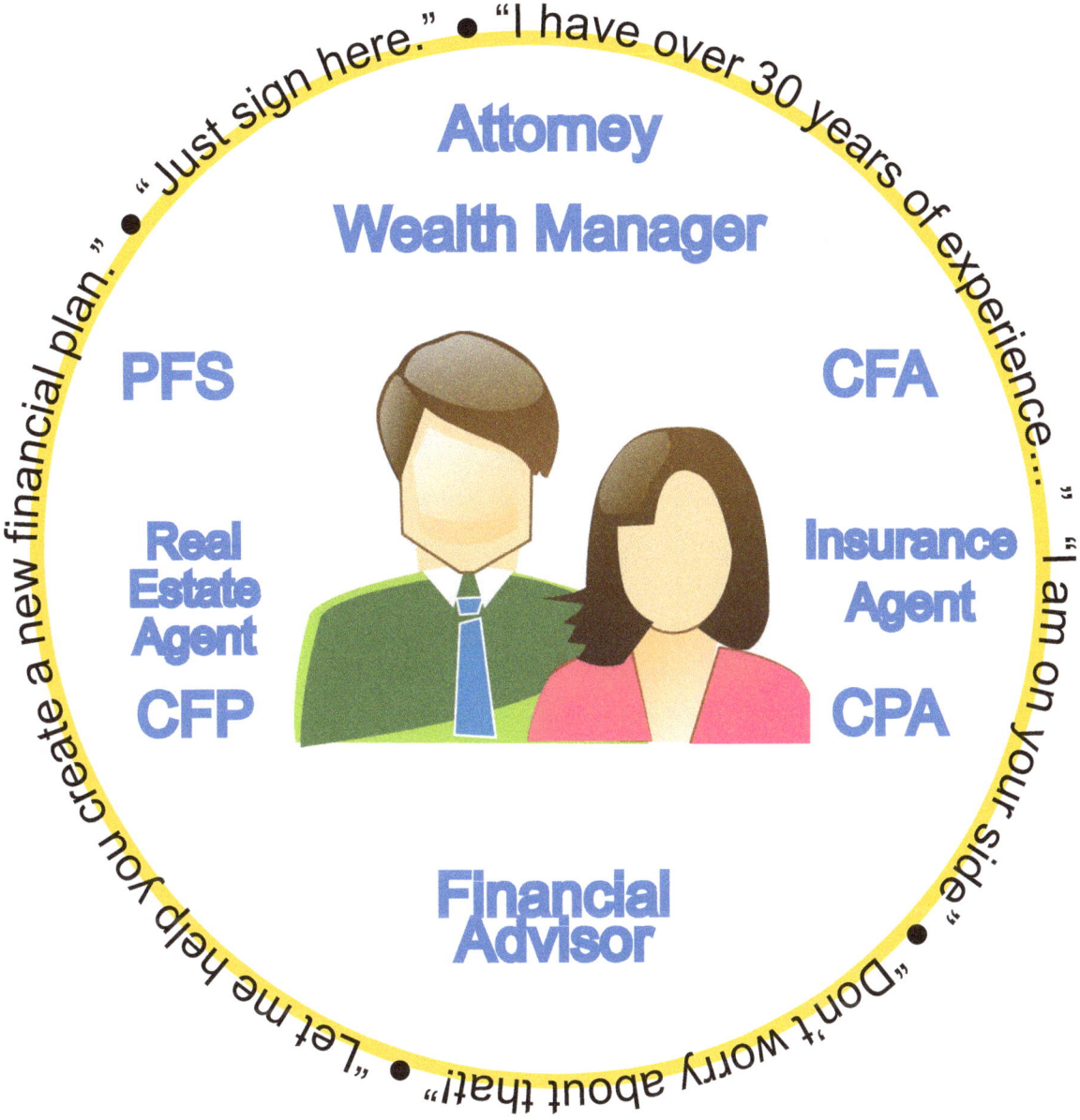

Course: A New Focus on Choosing the Right Professionals

Learn: How to choose the right professionals to help you create and implement a financial plan. An unethical or incompetent financial advisor, investment advisor, attorney, insurance agent, or realtor can derail your NEW. Learn the right questions to ask! We cover: attorneys, CPAs, PFS, CFPs, Real Estate agents, insurance agents, financial advisors, and wealth managers.

Who should attend: Everyone! You will undoubtedly need the help of professionals and you need to know how to select them.

Register: www.Essentialwealthconcepts.com

A NEW Focus on Legacy Planning and Transfers

THE FINAL CURTAIN PART I

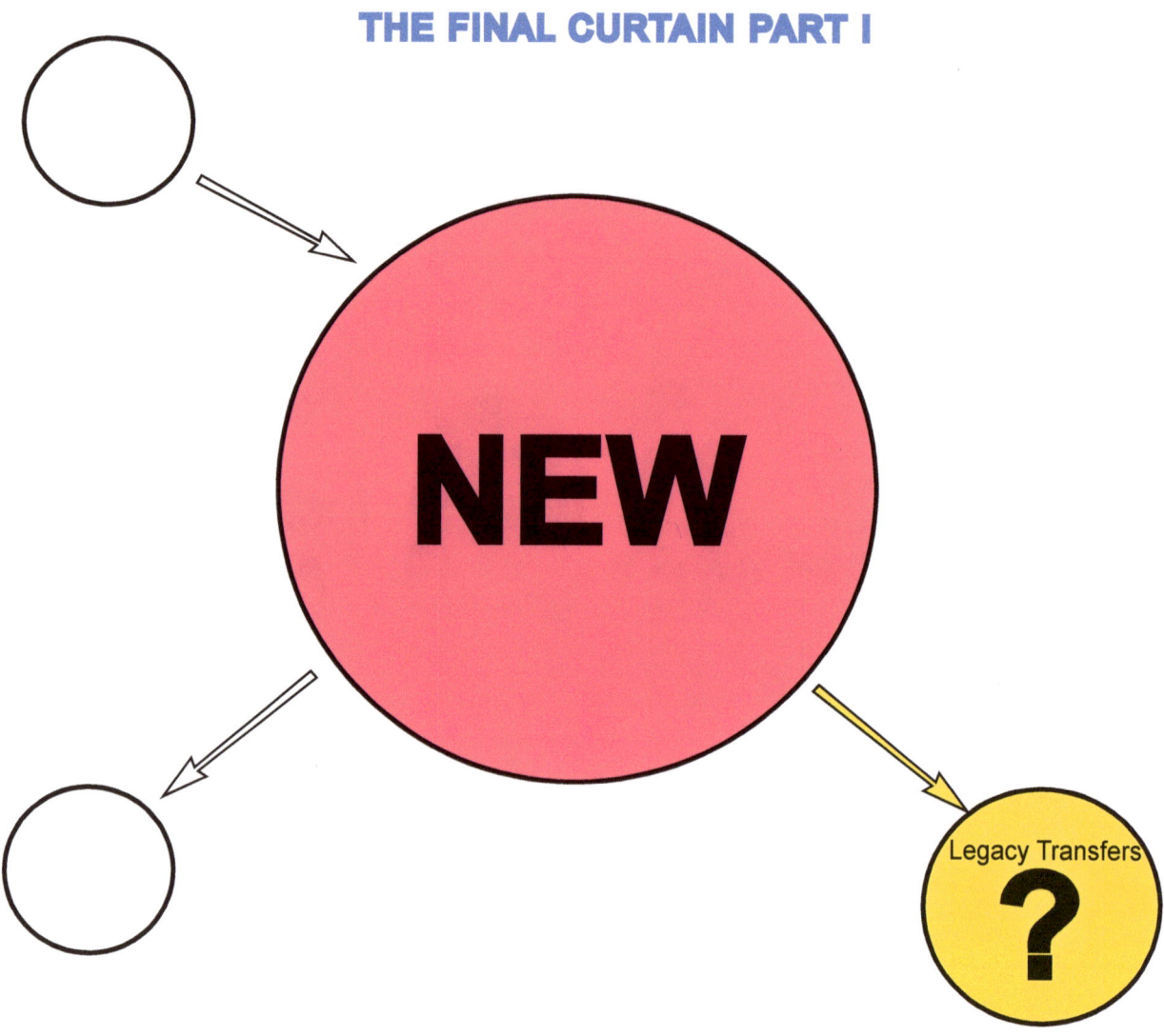

Course: A New Focus on Legacy Planning and Transfers

Learn: Very simply stated - you are not going to live forever and you want to make sure that your heirs, and not your attorneys, the IRS, or the state end up with your NEW. This book and online course will teach you about the documents that you need to have in place and things that you should think about before your final curtain. Remember, if you do not have a will the state has one written for you!

Who should attend: Everyone who plans on dying! Young and old! Everyone needs to know about the information contained in this book, you and your family will be glad that you read it.

Register: www.Essentialwealthconcepts.com

A NEW Focus on Estate and Gift Taxes

THE FINAL CURTAIN PART II

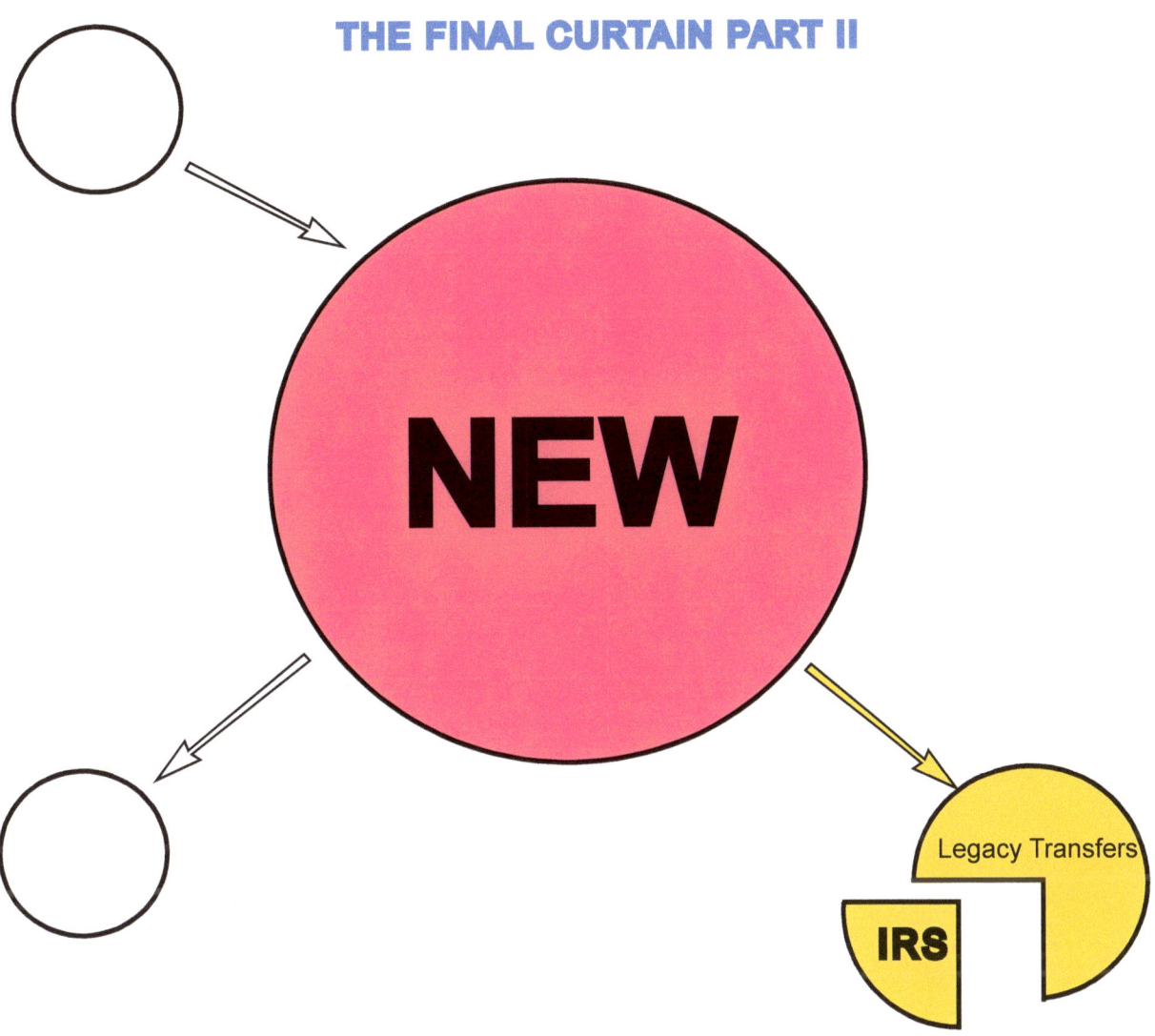

Course: A New Focus on Estate, Gift Tax and Generation Skipping Tax Planning

Learn: Death and Taxes – you can't escape them! This book and online course covers the fundamentals of how our estate, gift tax and generation skipping tax planning works and how to plan for the final curtain.

Who should attend: Anyone who has a NEW of more than 1 million dollars will benefit.

Register: www.Essentialwealthconcepts.com

MY NOTES

MY NOTES

_____

_____

_____

_____

_____

_____

_____

_____

_____

_____

_____

_____

_____

_____

_____

_____

_____

_____

_____

_____

Glossary

ADJUSTABLE RATE MORTGAGE (ARM) A mortgage whereby the interest rate can change prior to maturity depending on the changes of a particular index such as the COFI, LIBOR, MAT and CMT.

AMORTIZATION The gradual repayment of a debt over a period of time, such as monthly payments on a mortgage loan, where the payments cover interest and a portion of principal so as to reduce the balance to zero at the end of the term.

ASSET ALLOCATION An investment strategy used to balance risk and reward in your portfolio by investing in several different types of asset classes such as cash, stocks and bonds and other asset classes.

ASSETS What you own.

BOND LADDERING A strategy where a collection of bonds is purchased usually at the same time, whereby one bond will mature each year over a period of usually 10 years. As each bond matures, that money is reinvested in a new bond at current interest rates and becomes the last bond to mature in the future.

BONDS Loans that are debt instruments issued by the US Government, municipalities and corporations when they want to borrow money. Bonds consist of two parts, the principal amount (face value or par value) and coupon rate. (See PAR VALUE and COUPON RATE)

BUDGETING A process for identifying and planning the use of your cash inflows and outflows an essential tool for increasing your NEW; your financial road map.

CAPITAL APPRECIATION An increase in the value of a capital asset.

CAPITAL PRESERVATION the act of holding on to your wealth.

CARRYING COST The cost of maintaining an asset. For example on a house carrying costs would include mortgage payments, taxes, insurance and repairs.

CARRY-TRADE A financial strategy where money is borrowed at a low rate of interest in one country and invested at a higher rate of interest in another country.

CASH MANAGEMENT The process of managing one's inflows and outflows to make sure that the outflows do not exceed the inflows.

CASH RESERVE CRISIS FUND Money set aside and readily available for an emergency or unforeseen, unavoidable, expense.

CDs (CERTIFICATE OF DEPOSIT) A bank deposit that is held in cash by the bank and which pays a fixed interest rate until maturity. A penalty is usually assessed if the CD is "cashed in" prior to its date of maturity. The CD interest rate is higher than the interest rate on a money market account.

COLLATERAL An asset that is offered to provide security for a lender. If the borrower stops making loan payments, the lender can seize (foreclose on) the asset. This collateral reduces the lenders risk of loss.

COMPOUND INTEREST Earning interest on interest over time.

CONSUMER PRICE INDEX (CPI) Compiled monthly by the US Bureau of Labor Statistics, the CPI tracks the changes in the prices of basic goods and services. It is used to measure the rate of inflation and as a benchmark for making adjustments to a host of important things including adjustments to wages, Social Security payments and income tax brackets so that these benefits keep up with the purchasing power of the dollar.

COST-BENEFIT RELATIONSHIP Process of weighing the cost against the benefit which will be derived from using a strategy to make sure that it makes financial sense before going ahead with the expenditure.

COUPON RATE The amount of interest paid by a debt instrument (bond) per year expressed as a percentage of the original face value of the debt instrument.

CREDIT SCORE A measure of an individual's creditworthiness. Credit scoring involves a variety of factors including a history of default, the current amount of debt, and the length of time that the individual has made credit card or loan payments. Banks and other financial institutions may use a credit score to determine whether or not an individual is likely to default on a loan, mortgage or other debt.

DEBT MANAGEMENT A discipline that consist of three parts: the management of the principal repayment of your debt, the management of the interest on your debt and the management of your attitude and behavior towards debt.

DEBT PRINCIPAL The balance of money still owed on a loan at any given time.

DEFLATION The opposite of inflation, or a fall in the general level of prices of goods and services in an economy.

DEPRECIABLE GOODS Items that are consumed over a period of time. Examples include cars and boats etc.

DISTRIBUTIONS Cash outflows of any kind.

DIVERSIFICATION A strategy used to lower risk in a portfolio by investing in a wide range of asset classes along with different investment styles. Also known as "not keeping all of your eggs in the same basket".

FIXED RATE MORTGAGE Interest is fixed for the period of the mortgage. Monthly payments remain the same throughout the term of the loan.

FUNCTIONAL DEPRECIATION The loss in value of an asset over time due to normal wear and tear or obsolescence.

HARD OR REAL ASSET CLASSES Assets with intrinsic value like real estate or gold; Real assets explicitly exclude financial instruments. Many hard or real assets can keep up with inflation but usually have higher carrying costs and lower liquidity, than financial assets.

HYPERINFLATION Extremely rapid and out of control inflation.

INFLATION A rise in the general level of prices of goods and services in an economy over time. It is commonly measured by the Consumer Price Index (CPI) (See Consumer Price Index).

INFLATION-ADJUSTED RETURN The "real return" of an investment after accounting for the impact of inflation; Example: If you earn 7% on an investment when the inflation rate averages 3%, your inflation-adjusted return is 4%.

INTANGIBLE ASSET An asset which you cannot see but which can generate income. Examples include the increased earning power associated with a higher education or the good will of a business.

INTEREST The cost of borrowing money, computed to encompass 3 factors: the inflation rate, a risk premium, and a return for lending the money.

INTERMEDIATE TERM DEBT A loan that is usually financed and repaid in 3 – 10 years. Examples include bank or dealership loans for cars, boats, or furniture.

LIABILITIES What you owe.

LONG TERM DEBT A loan that is financed with over a period of 10 – 30 years. Examples include a mortgage on real estate.

MONEY MARKET ACCOUNTS There are two types, 1) bank money market accounts and 2) brokerage money market accounts which are in fact a liquid mutual fund. Both pay interest and both trade at $1 of value in or out.

NEGATIVE AMORTIZATION When the loan principal balance increases rather than decreases because the monthly payment is not enough to cover the interest on a loan.

NET WORTH Also known as equity or wealth. Sum of a person's assets less their liabilities.

NEW Stands for Net Worth, Equity, or Wealth. **NEW** is the sum of a person's assets less their liabilities.

PAR VALUE The stated or face value of a bond or other debt at issue. It is the amount that will be repaid at maturity.

PRE-QUALIFIED The amount that a financial institution estimates that it will lend to you, prior to buying real estate or another asset.

RATE OF RETURN The profitability of an investment expressed as a percentage of the total investment; Rate of Return = (Income - Cost) / Cost.

RISK MANAGEMENT The identification, measurement and assessment of your potential to incur a loss in a given situation. Risk management consists of implementing strategies that will minimize or mitigate the financial impact of a loss to your **NEW**.

Glossary

RULE OF 78 An accelerated method of computing interest on a loan.

SECURED DEBT Debt that is secured by an asset. This security usually results in a lower interest rate than other loans that offer no security to the lender.

SHORT TERM DEBT A loan that is usually repaid within one to three years.

SIMPLE INTEREST A way of computing interest where interest is calculated as a percent of the remaining principal amount of the debt only.

TAX DEFERRED INVESTMENT A savings strategy of even vehicle where investments can grow in a tax free environment such as a Traditional IRA, Roth IRA, 401K or annuity

UNSECURED DEBT Debt that is not backed with collateral. This increases risk of loss to the debtor and usually results in a higher interest rate than loans that offer collateral.

UPSIDE DOWN ASSETS Also known as "underwater". A situation in which one owes more on a loan than the underlying asset's current value. After the housing crash many homeowners owned upside down properties where they owed more on their mortgage than their homes were worth.

WEALTH ACCUMULATION The growth of your net worth. More than just "money in the bank", your net worth is the total value of your property, investments and all other assets less your debts.

WEALTH MANAGEMENT The combination of interrelated planning principles, strategies and services that help you accumulate and preserve wealth.

WEALTH PRESERVATION Holding on to your accumulated wealth and maintaining it in spite of changing economic conditions and life circumstances that surround you.

Appendix on

Retirement Vehicles
and Annuities

APPENDIX ON RETIREMENT VEHICLES AND ANNUITIES

- OVERVIEW

- EMPLOYER RETIREMENT PLAN AND IRA OVERVIEW

- TAX INFORMATION ON CONTRIBUTIONS TO YOUR EMPLOYER RETIREMENT PLAN AND IRAS

- TAX INFORMATION ON DISTRIBUTIONS FROM YOUR TAXABLE RETIREMENT PLAN

- DIVORCE NEGOTIATIONS AND TAXABLE EMPLOYER RETIREMENT PLANS AND IRAs

- QUALIFIED DOMESTIC RELATIONS ORDER (QDRO)

- QUALIFIED EMPLOYER RETIREMENT PLANS AND QUALIFIED IRAs - TAXATION AT THE OWNER'S DEATH

- RETIREMENT PLANS AND BENEFICIARY DESIGNATIONS AT THE OWNER'S DEATH

- STAY FOCUSED ON YOUR NEW FOR RETIREMENT

- HISTORY OF ANNUITIES

- SO, EXACTLY WHAT IS AN ANNUITY?

- TYPES OF ANNUITIES

- TAX DEDUCTIONS AND CONTRIBUTIONS MADE TO AN ANNUITY

- INSIDE OF THE TAX-FREE ENVIRONMENT OF ANNUITIES

- TAXATION OF WITHDRAWALS FROM AN ANNUITY

- DIVORCE, ANNUITIES, AND TAXES

- DEATH, ANNUITIES, AND BENEFICIARY DESIGNATIONS

- TAXATION AT THE DEATH OF THE ANNUITANT

OVERVIEW

Most investments usually pay either interest or dividends and this income is taxed in the year that it is paid to the owner. When investments appreciate and are sold at a capital gain, these gains are also taxed in the year that the investment is sold.

However, growing your **NEW** inside of an employer retirement plan, an individual retirement account or even an annuity, can be a powerful way to save because you can grow your investments inside of these investment vehicles in a tax free environment. The owner does not pay taxes until distributions are actually made!

Yes! Believe it or not, our Government gives us a "tax break" to encourage us to save for our retirement.

Consider this: You save $5,500 each year and invest it in an IRA at 7%. Over 20 years, the $110,000 you saved will more than double. This is how you increase your **NEW** - save and invest and let the magic of compound interest work for you!

YEAR	ANNUAL DEPOSITS	INTEREST	BALANCE
1	$5,500	$0	$5,500
5	$5,500	$1,709	$31,629
10	$5,500	$4,612	$75,990
15	$5,500	$8,682	$138,210
20	$5,500	$14,391	$225,475
Total:	**$110,000**	**$115,475**	**$225,475**

❀ The reason for focusing on retirement plans and annuities in the same FOCUS is because these investments share some similarities when it comes to who will end up with these assets when death occurs.

WARNING: Employer retirement plans and individual retirement accounts (IRAs) and annuities are not probatable assets. These assets are passed from the decedent to a beneficiary via a "beneficiary designation" signed by the owner. This beneficiary designation overrides a decedent's will..

EMPLOYER RETIREMENT PLANS AND IRA OVERVIEW

Employer retirement plans and Individual Retirement Accounts (IRAs) are a great way to save. Just about everyone should build their **NEW** by using the tax advantages offered under the United States tax code for contributing to and saving for their retirement by using these tax qualified plans and accounts!

Contributions to and the appreciation in employer retirement plans and IRAs during a marriage are generally considered marital assets and therefore become part of a negotiated settlement. Situations are common whereby, at the beginning of a marriage, one partner already has a substantial interest in an employer retirement plan or IRA. Absent an agreement to the contrary, contributions to and the appreciation of these assets during a marriage are also considered a marital asset.

The valuations of employer retirement plans and the future benefits that will be derived from these plans can be extremely complex but contrary to popular belief, because of modern computer software, they are relatively easy for actuaries to value.

There are numerous types of employer retirement plans and IRAs available and the IRS rules and regulations pertaining to both the contributions to and distributions from retirement plans are both extensive and complex. It is not the purpose of this book to dig in to the mechanics of how each type of plan functions or the pros and cons of having one plan versus another or even to advise you on what investments to hold inside of these plans. Instead, the purpose of this FOCUS is threefold:

1 To encourage you to use employer retirement plans and IRAs to the fullest extent possible to build your **NEW**.

2 To educate you so that you know how these assets will be "divvied up" in a divorce so that you can stay alert during your marriage and have enough fundamental knowledge to understand the issues you may face in a divorce. Further, it encourages you to seek professional help in order to receive your fair share of any retirement accounts floating around in the family during a divorce.

3 To educate you on what happens with employer retirement plans and IRAs when a marriage ends in death and how to protect yourself and your **NEW** should 'til death do we part' takes place.

RESOURCE: If you would like more in depth information on employer retirement plans and IRAs, the IRS has several publications on their website. You can access these online at IRS.gov and by searching for retirement plan publications. The information is extensive.

Talking to your tax professional about plan alternatives that are suitable for you is a very smart place to begin your search.

Appendix on Retirement Vehicles and Annuities

 TAX INFORMATION ON CONTRIBUTIONS TO YOUR EMPLOYER RETIREMENT PLAN AND IRAS

NEW BUILDING STRATEGY: Whether you are part of an employer retirement plan (think 401K type plan) or you own a traditional IRA or Roth IRA account, you should make every effort to maximize on your annual contributions. This is a rock solid way to build your **NEW** because your contributions will be able to grow in a tax free environment for your future retirement.

NEW TAX SAVING POINT: Contributions to most employer retirement plans and IRAs also offer a tax advantage. In the case of a traditional IRA account (but not Roth IRAs) contributions are deductible on your individual income tax return. In the case of your employer retirement plan your contribution AND the "employer match" contributions are not included in your Form W-2 income.

NEW TAX SAVING POINT: In the event of the death of one spouse, employer retirement plans and IRAs can be rolled over from the deceased spouse to the survivor without any tax liability issues.

NEW TAX SAVING POINT: The rule is a bit more complicated for employer retirement plans in a divorce setting. Although the equivalent of a tax free rollover can take place, it takes a Qualified Domestic Relations Order (QDRO) to accomplish this same task.

NEW BUILDING STRATEGY: If you are a part of an employer retirement plan such as a 401K plan where there is an annual "employer match" always make sure that you take advantage of the maximum match otherwise, you are leaving money on the table and hurting your **NEW**.

 TAX INFORMATION ON DISTRIBUTIONS FROM YOUR TAXABLE RETIREMENT PLAN

POINT: Distributions from both qualified employer retirement plans and qualified IRAs that were funded with pretax dollars are taxed at ordinary income tax rates. No one paid taxes on the amounts contributed to these plans and so when the owner of the plan starts taking distributions, income taxes are due. Distributions from Roth employer retirement plans and Roth IRAs are generally not taxable, as they were funded by "after tax dollars" although rules and limitations apply.

POINT: Generally, when distributions are made from an employer retirement plan or an IRA prior to the age of 59 ½, there is an early withdrawal penalty of 10%. Some special exceptions apply.

IRS code section 72(t) offers relief from this nasty 10% penalty rule. This code section allows a person to receive withdrawals before they are 59 ½ years of age if withdrawals are taken in equal annuity type payments.

EXAMPLE: You are 55 and just got a divorce. Your share of your spouse's IRA was $1.2 million. You are under 59 ½ but do not have enough income to live on and you need income NOW!

Under IRS code Section 72(t) you can take equal distributions from your rollover IRA without penalty; of course, rules apply. This rule is helpful when the family assets are skewed toward the retirement plans of one spouse.

POINT: Required minimum distributions (RMDs) begin no later than April 1st following the year that you reach the age of 70 ½. Here again, nasty penalties apply if you fail to take the distributions.

DIVORCE NEGOTIATIONS AND TAXABLE EMPLOYER RETIREMENT PLANS AND IRAs

BEWARE! THE TAX MAN WILL EVENTUALLY PAY YOU A VISIT!

The problem with qualified employer retirement plans and qualified IRAs is that when distributions are made to the owner or beneficiary these distributions are taxable at ordinary income tax rates.

- Consider this: $100,000 in a savings account is NOT the same as $100,000 in a qualified employer retirement plan or a qualified IRA.

- The $100,000 in the savings account is "after tax money". You can simply spend and enjoy it without worrying about the tax man!

- On the other hand, the $100,000 in a qualified employer retirement account or qualified IRA is worth much less because you may find yourself paying out up to 37% in federal income taxes plus applicable state income taxes each time you make a withdrawal!

It is vital that when you are negotiating a property settlement that you recognize the tax implications associated with qualified employer retirement plans and qualified IRAs and take the tax implications of each plan in to consideration. Hire someone capable to help you understand the tax implications associated with accepting these assets as part of your overall divorce settlement and relate this to how this decision will affect your **NEW** now and in the future. Watch out because there are both pros and cons!

Try to remember that when you are negotiating a divorce settlement that it is also important that you not only look at the property that you will receive net of income taxes but, it is also important that you take a hard look at the income that you need now or in the future and relate this back to the associated tax ramifications of the future "after tax income" which will be produced by each asset that you are thinking of accepting.

EXAMPLE: Distributions from a $100,000 qualified retirement plan will always produce taxable income payable at your highest income tax rate whereas $100,000 invested in a non-retirement brokerage account full of nice juicy dividend paying blue chip type securities may provide you with income at a much lower tax bracket.

Appendix on Retirement Vehicles and Annuities

NEW BUILDING STRATEGY: As long as there is not a prenuptial agreement in existence or a state law that would limit your right to share 50% in contributions to and the appreciation of the retirement plans of your spouse during marriage, there should be no reason not to encourage your spouse to fund their retirement plan to the fullest while you are married.

NEW BUILDING STRATEGY: In a divorce settlement, a young adult who does not need immediate income could end up better off by aggressively going after assets that can grow tax free for 10 years or more.

NEW BUILDING STRATEGY: In a divorce settlement, an older adult who will need income sooner rather than later may want to lean more towards a settlement skewed more towards the non-qualified brokerage account loaded with qualified dividend paying blue chips. The tax burden of this account maybe less punitive than a qualified employer retirement account or qualified IRA.

Consider both options. A good attorney or financial professional should be pointing these subtle differences out to you. Ask them about it!

Distributions from a Roth employer retirement plan or a Roth IRA account are free of federal income taxes because these retirement accounts were funded with after tax dollars. Rules apply!

QUALIFIED DOMESTIC RELATIONS ORDER (QDRO)

A QDRO is a court judgment, order, or decree made pursuant to a State Domestic Relations Order which establishes the rights of a spouse, former spouse, child, or dependent to an employer retirement plan.

The QDRO recognizes the right of an individual other than the plan participant to receive all or a portion of a participant's benefits under a qualified retirement plan.

This can be a real **NEW** life saver in a divorce situation.

What about taxes when the QDRO is split apart? Once a QDRO is in effect, the plan participant will NOT be taxed on rollover distributions from the retirement or pension plan that are made to the spouse or former spouse. However, the QDRO needs to be executed very carefully in order to conform with all of the IRS rules and regulations surrounding the distribution. This is one area to which the participant needs to pay very careful attention because it will be the participant who will be hit with the taxes if the mechanics of the QDRO fails!

NEW BUILDING STRATEGY: A QDRO can be expensive to draft and execute. Since you will be paying 50% of the costs of the divorce, be sure to take this into consideration when dealing with small plans.

QUALIFIED EMPLOYER RETIREMENT PLANS AND QUALIFIED IRAs: TAXATION AT OWNER'S DEATH

FUTURE SHOCK! THE TAX MAN CAN BITE TWICE!

Qualified employer retirement plans and qualified IRA accounts have a "built in" tax liability and do not enjoy a step up in basis at the date of death of the owner. Instead, if an estate tax return needs to be filed, these assets are included in that tax return at their fair market value as of the date of death of the decedent.

What about that "built in" tax liability? If withdrawals are made, income taxes will be paid by the designated beneficiary at ordinary income tax rates applicable to that beneficiary.

Wealthy individuals often chose to leave their retirement plans and IRAs to charities for the above reasons.

SPOUSAL BENEFITS: Employer retirement plans and accounts can be rolled over to a spousal IRA and the spouse can then treat the retirement account as his or her own. Unlike a divorce where a QDRO would be required for a qualified employer retirement plan to be rolled over to a spouse, the only requirement at death is that the spouse be the valid designated beneficiary of the employer retirement plan.

NON SPOUSAL INHERITED IRAs: Employer retirement plans and IRAs left to beneficiaries other than a surviving spouse have special distribution rules.

NEW BUILDING STRATEGY: Be sure to have a conversation with your aging parents and make sure that their beneficiary designations are in proper order. If you don't do this there could be a mess to clean up after they are dead!

RETIREMENT PLANS AND BENEFICIARY DESIGNATIONS AT THE OWNER'S DEATH

DO NOT SCREW THIS UP!

One more time! Individual retirement accounts pass to the beneficiary designated by the owner at the owner's death. If you are married, make sure that both of you make arrangements to have your beneficiary designations changed preferably immediately before you get married. This process does not take place automatically just because you get married.

ERISA governed retirement plans such a 401(k) plan may or may not pass automatically to a spouse. If the spouse is not the designated beneficiary, there may be limitations to the spouse inheriting the plan based upon the time that a couple has been married.

NEW BUILDING STRATEGY: The safest play is to make the changes in advance of your marriage or immediately thereafter. DO NOT WAIT!

 STAY FOCUSED ON YOUR NEW FOR RETIREMENT

Remember that the end game is to build your **NEW** for your future retirement needs and this means paying special attention to the tax implication of a future sale of or withdrawal from any asset that you accept in a divorce settlement AND also paying attention to the tax implications and tax quality of income from any asset that you accept in a negotiated divorce settlement.

Turn to case study # 4 to learn why you need to make pension/retirement decisions as a couple.

WHAT YOU NEED TO KNOW ABOUT ANNUITIES

 An annuity is a retirement vehicle and during divorce negotiations (without protection from a pre-marital agreement) it will surely be counted.

It is not the purpose of this focus to discuss in detail all of the different types of annuity products on the market instead the purpose is to provide the reader with broad general information about annuities in the areas of taxation, divorce and death.

HISTORY OF ANNUITIES

Annuities are nothing new. In fact, annuities date back thousands of years to the days of the Roman Empire and have a colorful history that has evolved since then.

The word "annuity" comes from the Latin word "annua" which means "annual stipend".
The Romans obviously had the same problems with retirement planning and worries about running out of money as we have today!

"I knew I should have invested in those gladiator ventures!"

Although today's annuity market is dominated by large insurance companies, it is worth mentioning that private annuities between related and non-related individuals have been used for hundreds of years to provide income diversification. In recent history they have also been used to avoid estate taxes by cleverly removing assets from an estate.

 This FOCUS on annuities will focus mainly on annuities sold by insurance companies.

🐚 SO, EXACTLY WHAT IS AN ANNUITY?

- An annuity is essentially a contractual agreement between two parties whereby one party promises to pay the other party (the owner) a certain defined financial benefits over a specified period of time.

- There are four parties in an annuity contract.

GUARANTOR/ISSUER: This is the party who promises to pay the benefits under the annuity contract.

OWNER: The owner of the contract is the person who purchases the annuity and pays the premiums to the guarantor. The owner is responsible for any taxes that are due. The owner can be the annuitant.

ANNUITANT: This is the person on whose life expectancy the annuity payments will be calculated by an actuary. As noted above, the owner and the annuitant are often one and the same person.

BENEFICIARY: This is the person who is designated to receive any assets or income stream left in an annuity at the death of the annuitant.

ANNUITY WARNING # 1

Payments made from the annuity contract are guaranteed solely by a "guarantor" entity (such as an insurance company) who promises to pay the owner of the annuity contract. If the guarantor fails financially or cannot make good on their promise to pay the owner of the annuity, then the owner is "out of luck". The contract owner may have to say adios and goodbye to those $$$ that they gave to the guarantor along with any income that they expected to receive in the future from the guarantor.

NEW PROTECTION STRATEGY: If you are going to invest in an annuity make sure that you don't choose just any company to provide you with the guarantee. Make sure that the guarantor is financially strong and that you choose a company that has a very high credit rating. Don't settle for anything less. Look for a guarantor/issuer that is rated Excellent, Superior, or Very Good by the rating agencies such as Fitch or A.M. Best. Even a high rating by these agencies cannot guarantee that the guarantor will fulfill their promises under the contract.

NEW PROTECTION STRATEGY: Be forewarned that annuities are commissioned products and can be sold to you by high pressure sales people. Annuities are complicated retirement products and you need to do yourself a favor and do extensive homework before buying any annuity. You should never buy an annuity of any type until you understand if an annuity is an appropriate retirement investment option for you and also that the annuity product itself is the best type of annuity option for your financial needs.

TYPES OF ANNUITIES

As mentioned previously, it is not the purpose of this focus to go in to the details of all of the hundreds of annuity products available on the market. However, consider the taxation of two major categories – fixed and variable annuities.

Annuities can be **FIXED** whereby the income to be received by the annuitant is a fixed amount paid monthly, quarterly or annually.

Fixed annuities can be immediate, meaning that they start immediately, or they can be deferred which means that the payment stream starts later on.

Annuities can also be VARIABLE whereby the income to be received by the annuitant is a variable amount based upon the performance of the underlying investment sub-accounts.

INDEXED annuities fit somewhere in between fixed and variable annuities and pay a guaranteed minimum payout, although a portion of the payout is tied to an index such as the S&P.

Annuity products keep evolving and some of the annuities offered today are quite creative in construction and offer numerous benefits such as long term care options. These options are called riders. Each rider carries with it an annual cost.

 TAX DEDUCTIONS AND CONTRIBUTIONS MADE TO AN ANNUITY

- Unlike employer qualified retirement plans and qualified Individual Retirement Accounts, there is no tax deduction available for contributions made directly to an annuity.

- HOWEVER, annuities, can be owned by qualified retirement plans or qualified IRAs and to the extent that the owner is making a tax deductible contribution to the qualified employer retirement plan or qualified IRA, the annuity inside of those assets ends up getting funded.

 INSIDE OF THE TAX-FREE ENVIRONMENT OF ANNUITIES

- Capital appreciation, dividends and interest income earned inside of an annuity also build up in a tax free environment and are not taxed until they are withdrawn.

- **NEW** BUILDING STRATEGY: Today's annuities can be used as an investment strategy to grow assets tax-deferred inside of of the annuity. This strategy may be appropriate for a person who has maxed out on contributions to their retirement plans and who want to save more in a tax free environment.

TAXATION OF WITHDRAWALS FROM AN ANNUITY

ANNUITY WARNING # 2

The insurance company usually imposes an early withdrawal penalty if funds are withdrawn from an annuity contract prior to the end of a surrender period.

Annuities are generally not liquid assets.

It is noteworthy that annuities usually allow a 10% penalty free withdrawal annually.

- When annuities are held inside of a qualified retirement account they are referred to as qualified annuities.

- When annuities are not held inside of a qualified retirement account they are referred to non-qualified annuities.

- Withdrawals from annuities are taxed as ordinary income unless part of the withdrawal represents a return of the owner's capital.

- Special rules are available for fixed annuities whereby each payment consists of both ordinary income and a return of capital based upon an "exclusion ratio" which is computed based upon the annuitant's age and life expectancy.

EXAMPLE: You purchased an immediate fixed annuity for $100,000 that will pay you $800 per month for the rest of your life. For purposes of taxes, each payment that you receive will consists of two parts based upon an exclusion ratio which is computed based upon your life expectancy. (1) A partial return of your capital and (2) ordinary income.

EXAMPLE: You also invest $100,000 in a non-qualified variable annuity which grows to $125,000. The $25,000 increase is a combination of capital appreciation of the underlying sub-account investments and dividends paid by the sub-accounts. After the surrender period of 7 years, you decide to take the $25,000 out of the annuity. The $25,000 is all taxed as ordinary income. There are no capital gains rates available for variable annuities. Withdrawals continue to be taxed as ordinary income until all income has been withdrawn from the annuity. After that point is reached further withdrawals will be treated as a return of capital.

NEW TAX SAVING STRATEGY: In the example above the owner could have annuitized the entire $125,000 and taken the payment over his or her lifetime. In that case, each payment received by the owner would have consisted of a combination of a return of capital and ordinary income. This strategy may have resulted in the owner paying the ordinary income portion of the annuity at a lower tax rate than having to include the $25,000 lump sum all in one year.

WITHDRAWALS AND THE 59 ½ YEAR RULE: Like qualified employer retirement plans and qualified IRAs, annuities have the same 10% early withdrawal penalty for investors who are under the age of 59 ½.

ANNUITIES AND REQUIRED MANDATORY DISTRIBUTIONS: These apply to annuities held inside of a qualified employer retirement accounts or qualified IRA only. There is a 50% penalty assessed upon the amount that should have been withdrawn if the owner fails to make these distribution.

NEW BUILDING STRATEGY: Required minimum distributions are NOT required by non-qualified annuity accounts.

 DIVORCE, ANNUITIES, AND TAXES

In a divorce, it is unlikely or it may even be impossible to change the ownership of an annuity deemed to be a marital asset. Equalization of the division of the marital assets will have to compensate for this. If you do end up as the owner of an annuity in a divorce situation from a tax perspective, the bottom line is that you will inherit the same tax consequences as if you were the original owner.

Be careful!

If you are the original owner of the annuity, be prepared to have to keep the annuity.

Even if a change in ownership of a marital asset annuity is possible, you may not want to accept the risk of taking over the ownership of an annuity belonging to your spouse.

This is a conversation that you need to take up with your lawyer and financial professional to help guide you because of the complex nature of annuities.

DEATH, ANNUITIES, AND BENEFICIARY DESIGNATIONS

ANNUITY WARNING # 3

Annuities are not probatable assets. Annuities are passed from the decedent annuitant owner to a beneficiary via a "Beneficiary Designation" signed by the owner. This beneficiary designation overrides the decedent's Will

---

When an annuity is initially sold, a designated beneficiary is named at inception and therein lays a potential problem.

Before you get married you should have a conversation with your fiancé to discuss his assets and your assets and preferably just before you get married you should both have the beneficiary designation changed on your employer retirement plans, IRAs, annuities and life insurance policies. Changes to beneficiary designations can be revoked and so if the marriage does not take place you can change the designation back to your mother!

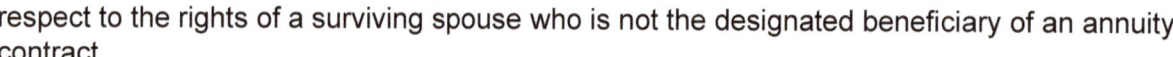

NEW PROTECTION POINT: Do not assume that once you are married that you automatically become the designated beneficiary of your spouse's annuity. States differ with respect to the rights of a surviving spouse who is not the designated beneficiary of an annuity contract.

NEW PROTECTION POINT: Remember that you do not want your in-laws to end up as the beneficiary of your spouse's annuity! You need that money to get over your grief. Work on getting those beneficiary designations changed in advance of when you say I DO.

TAXATION AT THE DEATH OF THE ANNUITANT

FUTURE SHOCK! THE TAX MAN CAN BITE TWICE!

Annuities have the same "built in" tax liability disadvantage as qualified employer retirement plans and qualified IRA accounts and do not enjoy a step up in basis at the date of death of the annuitant like other assets. Instead, if an estate tax return needs to be filed, these assets are included in that tax return at their fair market value as of the date of death of the annuitant.

What about that "built in" tax liability? When withdrawn, taxes will be paid by the designated beneficiary at ordinary income tax rates applicable to that beneficiary.

Wealthy individuals often chose to leave their annuities to charities if this is an option.

NEW BUILDING STRATEGY: Be sure to have a conversation with your aging parents and make sure that their beneficiary designations for any annuities that they may own are in proper order. If you don't do this there could be a mess for you to clean up after they are dead!

STAY FOCUSED: Remember it is all about building and protecting your **NEW**. Try to relate all financial decisions to your **NEW**.

Back to you!

CPSIA information can be obtained
at www.ICGtesting.com
Printed in the USA
LVHW070802160819
627830LV00003B/4/P